MW00462170

Bigfoot
in
Georgia

Jeffery Wells

Pine Winds Press

Pine Winds Press

An imprint of Idyll Arbor, Inc.

39129 264th Ave SE, Enumclaw, WA 98022

www.PineWindsPress.com

Cover Design: Thomas M. Blaschko

Pine Winds Press Editor: Thomas M. Blaschko

Photographs:

Pages 100, 106, 113, 114 by Wayne Ford

Pages 133-138 by Susan Prosser

© 2010 Idyll Arbor, Inc.

International copyright protection is reserved under Universal Copyright Convention and bilateral copyright relations of the USA. All rights reserved, which includes the right to reproduce this book or any portions thereof in any form whatsoever except as provided by the relevant copyright laws.

ISBN 9780937663172

Library of Congress Cataloging-in-Publication Data

Wells, Jeffery, 1974-

  Bigfoot in Georgia / Jeffery Wells.

    p. cm.

  ISBN 978-0-937663-17-2 (alk. paper)

  1. Sasquatch--Georgia. I. Title.

  QL89.2.S2W45 2010

  001.944--dc22

                                            2009030695

This book is dedicated to all the family members I have lost since my childhood, especially my grandmother Susie Taylor, grandfather W. F. Wells, and my great grandmother Freda Taylor. The values they instilled in me during my childhood have made me a stronger man. You three saints made sure I never forgot the value of a good education. I owe much to you and only wish you were here to help share in this work.

I also dedicate this book to all the aunts and uncles I have lost from my youth. The many family gatherings in South Georgia are filled with memories that are written on my soul.

Finally, this book is dedicated to my parents for their love and support. Thank you, mother, for making sure I never forgot my roots, and thank you, dad, for sacrificing so much to make sure I had a great education. This book is a product of your sacrifices as well.

Contents

Acknowledgements

There are a number of people that I would like to acknowledge for their support of me while I worked to complete this manuscript. First, I would like to thank Tom Blaschko and the staff of Pine Winds Press for offering me the opportunity to publish with them. In addition, I would like to thank Matt Pruitt for his encouragement, help, and his willingness to provide me with good information and contacts throughout the state. I would also like to thank Leverett Butts, Georgia Military College's Atlanta campus Humanities Department chair for offering advice and constructive criticism along the way. Also invaluable was Susan Prosser, Georgia Military College's Atlanta Campus library associate for helping me with the pictures and contact information. Your digging really helped me find out a lot of interesting things, Susan. I would also like to thank the dean of my campus, Roy McClendon, Jr., for encouraging me and allowing me to slip out a few minutes early some days to make those phone calls and set up interviews for this book. I also want to thank my best friend, Russ Gowin, for not letting me give up and making sure that I stayed focused as I toiled away at the computer working on each chapter. I also want to thank my friends and family for fostering my love of learning and writing and for continuing to ask me about my many research projects. Your interest in my work is much appreciated. Finally, I want to thank you, the reader, for being interested enough to open this book and pore through its pages of stories, sightings, and theories. By reading this book, you honor my work and commitment. Thank you very much!

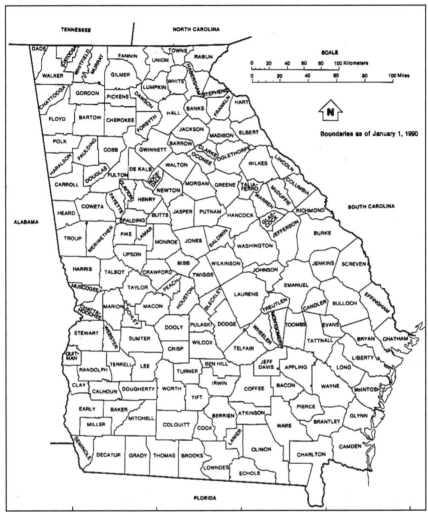

Figure 1: Georgia counties (U.S. Department of Commerce).

Introduction

Since the days of my boyhood, I have been interested in mysteries. As a historian and academic, I ponder questions like, "Did Oswald really kill Kennedy?" and "Where is Jimmy Hoffa's body?" a good bit. Teaching the second half of the general American history survey at the college level, I can say with a degree of certainty that these questions still interest first- and second-year college students today. The classes in which we talk about these ideas are a lot of fun.

Over the past few years, I have noticed that my students are interested in mysteries much like the ones that have interested me from since I was a young boy. In part one of my world history survey course, I always cover prehistory versus history. Inevitably, that leads the class to a discussion of the evolutionary stages of humans. We discuss *Homo habilus, Homo erectus, Homo sapiens, Homo sapiens sapiens* — and yes, Neanderthal Man. In the last few quarters, I have had students ask me questions about these ancestral humans, some of which look very much like one of the most famous objects of unsolved mysteries — Bigfoot. As such questions rolled in, students would be pleasantly surprised that I would be not only interested in discussing the alleged creature, but would in fact entertain their questions about it in relation to earlier humans, particularly Neanderthal Man.

To me, Bigfoot has always represented the "crown jewel" of unsolved mysteries. Bigfoot has it all: suspense, horror, science, science fiction, mystery, and a little bit of shock effect. While the Loch Ness monster is one of the most notable and famous unsolved cases where the realm of legend meets scientific inquiry, Bigfoot means so much more. Sea creatures, with Nessie as their flagship legend, are exciting too, but Bigfoot is supposed to walk like a human, use two hands like a human, eat some of the same kinds of foods as humans, and supposedly can be found in a lot of places, not just sometimes floating near the surface of some dark, murky lake. These creatures, if they exist, are said to live in the woods not far from human civilization. Some reports have them wandering dangerously close to urban areas. Famed Bigfoot researcher Robert Morgan even tells stories of reports he has received where these creatures roam into gardens planted by residents on the outskirts of towns and villages. There, they collect food and have even been known to leave things in return for what they have taken, such as objects made out of leaves and twigs. If these reports are indeed true, then these creatures could possibly teach humans a thing or two about gratitude and dignity.

As a young man, I ventured into the woods near my home and the surrounding areas a good bit. In all that time, I never heard any members of my family talk about a Bigfoot encounter, nor about seeing anything that remotely seemed like a Bigfoot or Sasquatch. In actuality, there was only one instance in the many times I went into the woods near my home in rural south Georgia where something happened that even sounds similar to what many today say indicates a Bigfoot encounter.

It happened around the summer of 1985, when I was 10. My uncle rented a house, barn, and small area of land from my grandfather so that he could train horses, his lifelong hobby and passion. Each summer, his grandsons would come to visit him at the horse farm, which was located right next to my boyhood home. During one of those summers, my uncle's grandsons asked me to join them as they wandered around on the horse trails my uncle and his stepson had marked out in the woods behind the farm and my house. We did that on several occasions, and I enjoyed it very much. I was a little nervous about being in those woods, because I had always heard about people getting bitten by snakes or stumbling upon coyotes, foxes, or even panthers, which my father said were present there.

My grandfather actually farmed the land, and he built several ponds on what was about 176 acres of farmland. From time to time, I had gone fishing with different family members in those ponds, but I had never really been on a walk through the deep part of the woods, which was natural forest and not planted pine. I am told this is the type of forest that these creatures commonly call home. So going on those horse trails was both exciting and a little scary for me. As we did this a few times that summer, I became more and more comfortable with those woods. On one outing, I decided to take my new radio with headphones. We used to call this kind of radio a Walkman. Although I cannot be certain, I think I lost my headphones on one of those hikes through the woods. When I returned home that afternoon, the radio portion was still clipped to my belt, but the headphones were gone. I thought that perhaps a limb or twig had caught the wire and pulled it, unknown to me, from my belt. I was told by my mother that I had better find those headphones because they were a gift that cost money, and losing them was a big "no no." I decided I had better not tell her about the trips through the woods, because that might compound the trouble I was going to be in if I were unable to find those headphones. So, I kept quiet about the hikes, and instead, I told her that I thought I might have put them down in my uncle's tack room at the horse barn. She told me that the next day I needed to retrieve them.

The next morning, I went back to the horse barn and told my cousins that we had to go back on the trails to find those headphones. They could not do it that day because they had been given the job of cleaning out a few of the stalls, after which they were to bathe and get ready to go somewhere with my uncle. One can only imagine my nervousness at not being able to go to the woods to find those headphones. But I could not go home without them, so I did the only thing I could and struck out on the trail we had walked the day before, albeit this time I was alone. This is when I came upon something that I now question. As I have recently been studying Bigfoot sightings in Georgia, I wonder if what I heard and experienced might be related to sightings of the creature in the state.

I had walked nearly halfway on the trail, still not having located the lost headphones, when I heard what sounded like a large animal rustling the leaves and moving through the woods in the distance, but not that far away. There was no foul odor, as is so common in Bigfoot sightings.

Since these woods were and still are full of large deer, I felt that more than likely that was the culprit.

However, as I continued walking along the trail, I heard whatever this was moving away. The sound of its footsteps reminded me of a horse's hooves hitting the dirt as it runs, but I had heard a lot of galloping horses and this did not sound quite the same. If this were a horse, then all of its hooves were hitting the ground at the same time, and everyone knows a horse does not run that way — I knew that just from being around them all the time with my uncle and grandfather. Whatever was running was loud. At that time, I became very nervous. I decided that I had better just wait around and let whatever it was get out of the area before continuing on, but that idea was about to be exposed as a really bad one.

Just as I had that thought and stopped to give whatever animal this was time to get away from the area, it let out a blood-curdling scream, two of them, actually. Living in that area, I was naturally familiar with the screams of bobcats, and my father and I had even heard a panther scream once at night, but this was very different. Those woods did not have bears, and in the years to come, I had the opportunity to hear the screams and roars of bears, and I do not remember the screams that day being the same as what I have heard since. In 1997, I even had the opportunity to hear the scream of a peacock, and while that kind of scream is unnerving as well, it still did not sound similar to what I heard that day in the woods.

After hearing the screams, I decided that it was in my best interest to turn around and get out of that area and the woods altogether. I did not waste much time, either. Now that I think about it, I recall getting out of the woods faster than I got into them. I believe that scream had

something to do with the pace at which I ran. I do remember being
scared for my safety and constantly looking over my shoulder as I ran
out of the woods, but I remember that the fear was what one often feels
when coming into contact with a wild animal. I do not remember being
afraid after the incident or having trouble sleeping, even though my
house was not at all far from those woods. I felt safe knowing that there
was a big field that separated my house from the woods, but the feeling
of anything unnatural or spooky never came over me, unlike what one
would feel about a ghostly encounter or after seeing a UFO.

I remember thinking that I needed to be careful if I ever went back
into the woods, but since I did not go alone except for that one time, I did
not feel as if there was any immanent danger. Looking back, I now
realize that the idea of Bigfoot never crossed my mind, and if memory
serves me, I think I chalked this incident up to a "there are dangerous
wild animals out in those woods" type of idea. I did not give it much
thought in the years afterwards.

From time to time after that, I managed to find different books and
articles on Bigfoot sightings in the United States. I saw the
Patterson/Gimlin film on some cable program where the hosts were
trying to prove that the film was a hoax and that the creature was nothing
more than a man in a suit. Other sightings and pictures caught my
attention, and my interest grew. However, one thing I recognized was
that other than a few sightings in Florida of what they now call the Skunk
Ape, all of the big sightings were in the Pacific Northwest, and this was a
world away from me in Georgia. Reading the materials that were
available to me, I still had not given any thought to the screams I had
heard as a young man in those woods behind my house. As I kept reading
about this elusive creature, I felt certain that Georgia was the last place it

would be; in my mind, there was no such thing as a Georgia Bigfoot. Whoever he was, he was roaming through the woods in Washington and Oregon, not in the woods and fields of southeast Georgia.

In 1998, I began my teaching career. By 2004, I had taught high school English and social studies in several Georgia high schools. That year, I was teaching a research and writing course at a private high school in central Georgia. As part of the class requirements, students were required to submit an original research paper on a topic that interested them and that involved an unsolved mystery. One student who was quite the avid outdoorsman asked my permission to do a research paper on Bigfoot. I gave him permission, but mentioned that there were a lot of sources out there, since the topic was already quite broad. He surprised me when he asked me a question that has a direct relation to the writing of this book: "Do you think there have been any sightings of that thing in Georgia?" Surprised by his question, as well as by the possibility of such a creature residing in the Peach State, I told him that I did not think there were, but that he should investigate and report back to me. The young man had his research topic. Secretly, I felt that it would be only a matter of days before he came back to me asking to change his topic due to lack of sources, but that was not to be.

He did return, but not with a request for a different topic. On the contrary, he had found several sources that included sightings in Georgia. I was more than shocked. Also in his list of sources he included several interviews he had conducted with hunters who had seen strange things in the woods of central and southeast Georgia. I remember being quite shocked that he had found so many sources. When I read the paper late one evening while trying to get caught up on grading so that I could return papers to the students, I felt a bit unnerved, especially when I realized that sightings had taken place right here in the Peach State and not just far, far way in the Pacific Northwest. I remember the title of his paper being "Georgia Bigfoot Sightings." The name itself was enough to spark interest.

For the next few years, I tried reading what I could about Bigfoot, not exclusively in Georgia, but in general. As time went by, I began seeking out sightings in Georgia, first by looking at newspaper reports of those in the state who reported encounters with what they thought was the creature, or at least strange experiences that trained researchers claimed were Bigfoot-related. To my surprise, there were several Internet databases that included sightings from Georgia. The largest was The Bigfoot Field Researchers Organization, whose website can be found at http://www.bfro.net. Currently, the site lists over fifty-five sightings in Georgia; however, these are sightings that are deemed credible enough to publish for the public. This does not include reports that are received by the organization, but for whatever reason are not released from their archives. The sightings in Georgia are mainly from north Georgia counties, but reports can also be found about southeast Georgia near the coast, as well as western and middle Georgia. The BFRO was founded in 1995, and is said to have the worldwide web's most extensive database of Bigfoot sightings in the U.S. and Canada.

In addition to the BFRO, there are sightings posted at the site for the Gulf Coast Bigfoot Research Organization. At the time of my research for this book, this organization listed over twenty-five sightings from Georgia. Founded in 1997, the GCBRO, whose site can be found at http://www.gcbro.com, focuses mainly on sightings reported in the South; however, the group does take sighting reports from states all over the nation, and they, like the ones from the American Southeast, can be found in the database on the GCBRO website. I have included and discussed some of the more interesting sightings from both the BFRO and GCBRO in the chapter on these two organizations and their research. Other databases do exist that list sightings in Georgia, including http://www.bigfootencounters.com, the Alliance of Independent Bigfoot Researchers, and Sasquatch Research Initiative. I have included a few sightings in Georgia from these databases and sites, as well.

Although the GCBRO, BFRO, Bigfootencounters.com, and others were all valuable to my research, perhaps none were as valuable as Georgia Bigfoot. Their website is http://www.georgiabigfoot.com. While it is not an official organization like GCBRO and BFRO, Georgia Bigfoot and some of its leading members provided me with one of the most remarkable pieces of evidence and sighting reports that exist in the state and in its history — the Elkins Creek cast. In terms of Georgia sasquatchery, as the field of research has oftentimes been called, the Elkins Creek cast is akin to the Roswell Crash for UFO researchers or the Patterson/Gimlin footage of 1967 to Bigfoot/Sasquatch research in general. I have devoted an entire chapter to Georgia Bigfoot and the Elkins Creek cast.

To help piece together the events surrounding this piece of evidence and its discovery, I was able to interview Steve Hyde and Mike Bankston of Georgia Bigfoot, the current operators of the website. It was also this cast that led me to Dr. Jeffrey Meldrum, famed Bigfoot researcher, frequent guest on programs produced by the Discovery Channel and the History Channel, associate professor of anatomy and anthropology at Idaho State University, and affiliate curator of the Idaho Museum of Natural History. In a phone conversation, Dr. Meldrum discussed the Elkins Creek cast and what he knew of Georgia sasquatchery. For an overall understanding of the Bigfoot/Sasquatch creature, I also read Dr. Meldrum's book, *Sasquatch: Legend Meets Science*. In addition, *Sasquatch: The Apes Among Us* by John Green, *The Scientist Looks at the Sasquatch* by the late Dr. Grover Krantz of Washington State University, and *Bigfoot! The True Story of Apes in America* by Loren Coleman all helped build my foundational knowledge about the alleged creature so that I could better understand how sightings from Georgia fit into the overall picture.

Once I had pored over this material, I started looking for historical sources that might reflect on when and where this creature had been sighted in the 1800s and 1900s in Georgia, since most of the database materials from BFRO, GCBRO, Georgia Bigfoot, and other more limited databases, chronicled sightings from the last decades of the twentieth century and what years we have already seen in the twenty-first century. On a few occasions there were references to sightings from before 1900 in some of these databases, but not many. Much to my chagrin, I did not find very many published sources from the nineteenth and early twentieth century among Georgia's newspapers. In chapter 3, I speculate on a few theories that might explain why this is the case. However, there have been more than a few newspaper accounts of Bigfoot sightings in Georgia in the last twenty-five years. This led me to perhaps the most notable journalist in the state who has written about the Bigfoot phenomenon, Wayne Ford of the *Athens Banner-Herald*. In addition to reading and analyzing the articles Ford wrote on sightings in Georgia, I was able to interview him by phone, where he told me many things about his research, writings, and personal field trips into the Georgia wilderness looking for the creature.

After pondering the state of newspaper accounts in the 1800s and early 1900s in Georgia, I began to wonder if perhaps the Cherokee and Creek Indian nations, part of the Mississippian culture living in the state before and shortly after the arrival of Europeans, might have legends and myths in their popular lore indicating they had indeed run into such an animal in the fields and forests of what is now Georgia. One source to which I turned was the book *Myths of the Cherokees* by the noted anthropologist James Mooney, who spent a great deal of time studying the culture of America's native tribes. To help further my understanding of Cherokee and Creek myths and legends, I visited the Ocmulgee National Monument in Macon, Georgia to speak with on-site rangers and experts about the Creeks, and New Echota State Park for a glimpse into Cherokee culture. Both trips proved valuable and insightful.

As I gathered all of these documents, books, and pieces of evidence, I was quick to realize that there was no lengthy work about Georgia Bigfoot/Sasquatch sightings and the history of the phenomenon in the state. Jim Miles in *Weird Georgia* references a few sightings in Georgia, but the book is more or less about strange events, people, places, and happenings in the state and not much focus is placed upon the Georgia Bigfoot. Additionally, in his book *Bigfoot across America,* Philip L. Rife mentions sightings in Georgia, but devotes less than three pages to the state and its history of encounters. In his work, Rife divides the nation into regions, Georgia being in chapter four about the Southeast. In that chapter, the reader will find far more about Bigfoot sightings in Alabama and Florida than in Georgia.

Because of the dearth of information in print on the history of Bigfoot in Georgia, I felt that it was important that a new contribution be made. Due to the multitude of sightings and encounters reported to the various organizations backing research and tracking, much research and fieldwork is being carried on in the state today. So I concluded that the legend of Bigfoot was alive and well in Georgia, and indeed was causing many people out there to spend valuable time and money in an attempt to find it. While the debate about its existence goes on and will for quite some time, clearly the evidence proves that there is a history of sightings, encounters, and research centered on Bigfoot in Georgia. If that is the case, and certainly it is, then this story needs to be told. Out of that sentiment, my research was born.

I hope that, above all, my work will make readers take an objective look at what evidence has been collected and what research is now going on, so that each and every one of them can make a judgment as to whether or not Georgia Bigfoot exists. As I told a researcher that I interviewed by phone, my job is merely to present the story through past and present history — proving that the creature does or does not exist is up to someone else entirely. After reading this work, you will have to make a personal decision about the evidence.

1
What is Bigfoot?

The field of cryptozoology, the science dealing with animals not yet recognized and chronicled by science, includes the study of Bigfoot, also known as Sasquatch. It is perhaps the most popular cryptid in the field. This begs the question "What is Bigfoot?" and also invites a discussion of when the animal began to appear in the annals of American folklore, myth, and legend.

There are literally hundreds of books written about Bigfoot. It would take just a few moments in a public library to find that there are dozens of books about Bigfoot in the juvenile section, as the topic has also been one of interest and delight to younger readers for generations. Historians, folklorists, anthropologists, zoologists, and biologists have all written about the elusive creature, and many of their books recount the history of the phenomena across the country.

The word 'Bigfoot" seems to be a twentieth-century designation. According to Loren Coleman in his book *Bigfoot: The True Story of Apes in America,* "The direct labeling *Bigfoot* did not occur until a man named Jerry Crew appeared at a northern California newspaper office with the plaster cast of a large humanoid footprint." It was after this that a reporter for the *Humboldt Times* named Andrew Genzoli first coined the term Bigfoot, which he used in an article he wrote and published in the paper on October 5, 1958.[1] One must understand that simply because the term Bigfoot was not used prior to 1958 does not mean that there was no Bigfoot activity before that time. As the many books written on the subject by authors like Coleman, Dr. Jeff Meldrum, Dr. Grover Krantz, journalist John Green, and biologist Dr. John Bindernagel reveal, Bigfoot has quite a solid history in both Canada and the United States, a history that certainly predates 1958.

Bigfoot is also sometimes called Sasquatch. The word itself was first used by J.W. Burns, an Indian-agent who also taught on the Chehalis Indian Reservation. The word is a derivative of the Native British Columbian term used to describe hairy giants.[2] One anthropologist, Thomas Buckley, asserts that Bigfoot/Sasquatch was a source of some concern to natives in northwestern California even before aboriginal times. As evidence of this, the Karok Indians told stories of beings they called "upslope persons." They described them as hairy and large. They were purported to have lived in rocky dells in the mountains of California.[3] History tells us that the natives of the Pacific Northwest have believed in Bigfoot for quite a long time. Their legends include tales about giant men near Mount Shasta, as well as stick men of the Washington mountains.[4]

Perhaps the first European to see Sasquatch or Bigfoot was the Norse explorer Leif Erikson, who arrived in what would later be called the "New World" over a thousand years ago. Erikson and his crewmates claimed to have seen strange creatures that they described as ugly, dark, and hairy; they also said that the creatures had big black eyes.[5] Through the years, there were a number of sightings by European settlers and American citizens, but one of the more famous sightings in America actually comes from a book written by Theodore Roosevelt, former president of the United States.

According to Roosevelt in his book *Wilderness Hunter*, a hunter named Bauman and a friend were in the mountains close to Wisdom River near the Idaho-Montana border on a hunting trip. One day, they returned to their camp to find that something had destroyed the lean-to they were using as a shelter and had also rummaged through their belongings and gear. They found footprints in the camp indicating that the intruder who had wrecked their campsite had been of the two-legged kind. Later that night, Bauman was awakened, and in the darkness he saw a dark shape and smelled a foul odor. He took his rifle and fired at it. This must have riled the creature, for the next day, returning to their camp after hunting, they again found that their lean-to had been destroyed. This was too much for the campers, and they decided to abandon the area. As they began to collect their hunting traps, they decided to split up. Bauman continued collecting traps while his friend returned to their campsite. A few hours later, Bauman entered the camp to find it very quiet. Upon further inspection, he found his friend's body nearby, lifeless and with fang marks in the throat.[6]

The next encounter, which happened to Canadian Albert Ostman in 1924, involved a kidnapping at the hands of a family of Sasquatch. While a number of people think that the story is false or embellished, it has been a staple in the history of Sasquatch encounters ever since Ostman decided to tell his story.

Ostman, a lumberjack, decided to take a vacation to prospect for gold. While traveling through the Canadian wilderness, he was accompanied by an Indian guide who told him the story of Bigfoot before turning back and leaving Ostman to continue the journey on his own. On the third night out, Ostman was picked up as he slept in his sleeping bag. He could not be sure but felt that he was carried through the forest by a large hairy creature for about three hours. At the end of that three-hour period, it dropped him to the ground, still in his sleeping bag.

At dawn, he was finally able to see his captors. Ostman said that the beings looked more human than apelike; there were four of them. The large male looked to be about eight feet tall, with large arms and legs. His fingernails looked to be short and broad, and he was totally covered with hair, as were the other three: a larger female, a smaller male, and a small female. Ostman felt that this was a family unit. It appeared that the family slept in a cave on what looked like blankets made of cedar bark and dry moss. The animals did not harm Ostman, but they seemed to observe him really closely. Ostman was finally able to escape when the large male took an interest in his dipping tobacco. The creature ate the powdered substance and it made him sick, for he screamed in pain. Ostman took this opportunity to break for an opening in the nearby canyon wall. Although the female tried to pursue him, he took the gun he had been keeping and fired a shot over her head, an act that sent her fleeing back to the safety of their cave. Ostman, afraid that people would think he was lying, was reluctant to tell his story until 1957, when there seemed to be a rash of Bigfoot sightings and activities.[7]

Ostman was right. There did seem to be an outbreak of Bigfoot activity in the late 1950s. In addition to the term Bigfoot being coined in that year, the first set of Bigfoot track casts were made. Also, what might be the first photographs of Bigfoot surfaced. Carrie Carmichael writes about the story in her booklet *Bigfoot: Man, Monster, or Myth?* published in 1977. She writes, "The *San Francisco Chronicle* published a photograph of what may have been a Bigfoot. In the late 1950s, a weather-beaten woodsman named Zack Hamilton brought some photographs to the newspaper's offices. He said he had been followed by a hairy creature while he was hiking in the Three Sisters Wilderness area in the state of Oregon. Mysteriously, Zack Hamilton never went back to the newspaper office. Nothing more is known about him and his photographs."[8] Perhaps Hamilton was behind a hoax, or perhaps he was too afraid to come back and get in the middle of the publicity and certain ridicule that would follow his turning over the photos. Whatever the case may be, it is the first time on record that anyone tried to turn in photos of an alleged Bigfoot to a major newspaper.

The late 1950s did see, however, a number of things that are still part of the commonly accepted history of Bigfoot. First, on August 27, 1958, a road builder named Jerry Crew would return to the worksite in Bluff Creek, California, where he was part of a crew that was building a road through the thick forests of northern California. As Crew strolled to the machine he operated, he noticed large footprints in the dirt. He investigated further and saw a whole line of footprints leading to his bulldozer. The tracks were quite large, indeed larger than any he had ever seen. Immediately, he noticed how much larger the tracks were than his own, and he even attempted to walk in the tracks but could not because the stride was too large and the tracks were too far apart. He immediately reported the incident to the crew foreman, Wilbur Wallace, who recounted to Crew his own strange story where something or someone quite large had removed a fifty-five gallon diesel container from a job site on which he worked. The workman who discovered them missing reported that he followed a set of tracks into the woods to a place where the drum must have been set down. There, he discovered that the bright orange drum had been thrown over the ravine. There were no visible snapped twigs or broken fauna in the area, so the workmen surmised that the entity must have carried the drum and not rolled it, as that would certainly have left an imprint and evidence of the roll. Wallace felt that whatever had done this was huge, and was perhaps the same type of thing that had made those large footprints Crew found. The two decided to keep their stories quiet so as not to alarm the workmen on the road crew.[9]

The issue was not resolved, for on October 1st of that year, Crew once again saw tracks. After he had reported this new find, some of the crew found out and two workmen quit on the spot and eventually moved their families out of the mountains. Because some people were laughing at him, Crew decided to make a plaster cast of one of the footprints, and showed it to the other workers. Not long afterwards, Crew and his plaster cast were photographed and placed on the front page of The *Humboldt Times*, and the buzz began.[10]

Bluff Creek would again be the site of another huge part of the Bigfoot story. In October 1967, Roger Patterson, a rodeo rider from Yakima, Washington, and his expedition partner, horse rancher Robert

Gimlin, filmed what they believe to be a female Sasquatch near a creek in the Bluff Creek area of northern California. Roger Patterson had become very interested in the topic of Bigfoot after reading an article written by Ivan Sanderson. After traveling to Bluff Creek in 1964 to make a plaster cast of prints there, Patterson decided to return in 1967 to try to collect more evidence. Indeed he did, and the world was left with the now-famous Patterson-Gimlin footage shot on October 20, 1967.[11]

The Patterson-Gimlin footage is perhaps the crown jewel of Sasquatch evidence; no book on the history of the animal and its sightings can be written without some mention of it. It has been examined, debated, dissected, discussed, and analyzed by scientists, Bigfoot researchers, creators of documentaries, film historians, movie producers and directors, costume specialists, experts in biomechanics, and photographers for the last forty years. There have been stories about how it is a hoax, even coming down to a man, Bob Heironimus, who claimed that he was wearing the suit and was asked to do so by Roger Patterson. So far, no concrete proof of that claim has come to light, although writer Greg Long in his book *The Making of Bigfoot: The Inside Story*, claims that there is. According to Long, in 2002, Phillip Morris of Morris Costumes in North Carolina claimed that he had *manufactured* a gorilla costume for use in the now-famous footage at Bluff Creek. Morris never talked about his alleged involvement in the event until the 1980s, but he admitted to it on a Charlotte, North Carolina, radio show on August 16, 2002. He claimed that he would have talked about it much sooner, but did not want to bring negative repercussions to his business.[12] Others have claimed that famed costume designer for the movie series *Planet of the Apes*, John Chambers, designed the suit. Chambers himself denied having been involved with the Patterson-Gimlin footage and said before his death that he knew nothing of the suit. According to Chambers himself, he was not talented enough to have made a suit that convincing.[13]

Because the Patterson-Gimlin footage has never been proven a hoax and most Bigfoot researchers accept it as legitimate (as do a number of noted scientists) it is most often used to illustrate what a Bigfoot looks like. The image on the film is undoubtedly that of a female creature, because breasts are clearly visible in the film. The animal walks upright on two feet (bipedal) and has arms that extend below its waist. In addition, it seems to have a pointed head, often called a sagittal crest. The animal appears to be covered in dark hair and has a wide stride. These are all things that have come to be associated with Bigfoot.

However, this film, like the other evidence mentioned above, was shot in northern California, which is considered a part of the Pacific Northwest. For all intents and purposes, this is where most people consider the home of Bigfoot to be. However, as historical evidence suggests, Bigfoot lives in other places as well, and it is the subject of this book to show the historical evidence that Bigfoot also calls the state of Georgia home.

Since the history of the creature presented thus far seems to reflect on characteristics of the creature as it exists in the Pacific Northwest, the question could be asked, "So what is the *Georgia* Bigfoot?" It might seem erroneous to turn so quickly away from this general history of Bigfoot in America at this point, but any curious person who wants to know about the plethora of sightings of Bigfoot in America can turn to a number of books and magazines to find such information. In addition, there are many books out there that focus primarily on the biological, morphological, and behavioral aspects of Bigfoot, but since there is no current literature out there on these animals in Georgia, it is wise to ask these same questions specifically about the Georgia Bigfoot. To do that, it is the better part of wisdom to turn to those who have been studying the Georgia creatures exclusively for details and information.

One of the individuals who is the most knowledgeable about Bigfoot in Georgia is Matt Pruitt, a native of the north Georgia mountains, an area that many say is one of the main homes of the Georgia Bigfoot. Pruitt got involved in Bigfoot research in 1999 at the age of 17.[14] For quite some time before this, Matt had been an enthusiast in paranormal and mysterious activities. As a native of north Georgia, he felt especially drawn to ghost stories, local folklore, and mountain legends. One particular legend in which he became interested was about a Cherokee witch doctor said to be able to shape-shift.[15]

Legend has it that in White County, in an area that Pruitt knew quite well, there was a wealthy man who owned a large home and quite a bit of land. On this land in a cabin in the woods lived a Cherokee witch doctor that the man had brought to his home place for unknown reasons. As with similar tales, myths and stories abounded about what the witch doctor could do. According to some, she could change shape at will. One of the more popular legends that Pruitt heard growing up was that she could change herself into a dog-like monster that was very hairy and could walk upright, and indeed, such an animal had been seen in this particular area of White County on numerous occasions at that time. In fact, Pruitt recounted a story to me: Some of his friends were so intrigued by the legend that they set out to find the fabled witch doctor's cabin in the woods of White County in the 1970s. They were successful in finding the cabin and decided to stay the night there so that they could see the ghost of the witch doctor as she shape-shifted into the upright walking dog creature. His friends got their wish and saw the creature. After getting involved in Sasquatch research, Pruitt believes that the legend of the shape-shifting witch doctor is just that, a legend. In fact, he feels that what residents of White County, including his friends, were actually seeing was Bigfoot.[16]

Another mountain legend that Pruitt heard as a young man growing up in White County was the legend of the Whistle Monsters. The legend included stories of people hearing strange noises like beings whistling in the woods. Many thought that these strange and supernatural occurrences were these monsters communicating with each other. Now, Pruitt makes sense out of this by attributing these "whistle" sounds to the sometimes high-pitched calls and whistles of the Sasquatch.[17]

It was legends like these that led Pruitt into the woods. In fact, he and a group of friends decided that they would explore the woods near the alleged location of the witch doctor's cabin, much as his friends had done previously. He and his group packed up their gear, fully intending to stay the night on the side of the mountain where the property was located; they wanted to find that cabin and see if the legend was true. As they were walking up that mountainside, they were frightened by limbs being broken and thrown, screaming, wood-knocking, and the glowing red eyes of animals in the woods. Pruitt and his friends were so alarmed that they thought the wood-knocking sounded as loud as gunshots. They were all very scared, especially at the screams. Eventually they figured out that the vegetation they heard being broken was actually trees being pushed down; there also seemed to be an animal in the distance doing the screaming they heard. They decided to leave the area and go to Pruitt's mother's house. At the time, no one in the group knew what they were up against; they thought that the place was just haunted. Now, he fully realizes that this was his first encounter with the Georgia Bigfoot.[18]

A few years later, Pruitt and a few more friends were camping in Union County and heard something walking along the tree line. Later in the night, they heard the animal leave the woods and start walking through the meadows. It seemed to be approaching their tents and campfire. He alerted the other members of the group, resulting in one of them yelling at him to go to sleep. This loud outburst caused the animal to scream loudly and retreat back into the woods. It sounded like a truck moving in the brush. At that time, all of the group got up, frightened by what they had heard and experienced. They did end up laughing when the danger had passed, but, in hindsight, Pruitt feels that this was a Sasquatch approaching their camp.

A while later, Pruitt stumbled upon the Bigfoot Field Researchers website and read an article about what a Sasquatch was; the article was penned by Henner Fehrenbach. He realized that he had indeed encountered these things on the earlier occasions. He began reading materials on the Sasquatch and tried to learn as much as he could. At that time, there were no BFRO investigators in Georgia, and much of what had been printed on the site about Georgia had been reported by the group's leader Matthew Moneymaker, as well as others who were not in Georgia. It was at this time that he began doing his own research in the woods. Although he was not really doing proper research, he had an awareness of what the creatures were and how they behaved when humans were near.

Until 2006, he had not met many people doing such research in the state. One individual, John Hall, an independent Bigfoot researcher, did meet Pruitt shortly after he became interested in the subject, and Pruitt credits him with being the one who introduced him to active field research. Nonetheless, in the meantime he was reading all he could about Bigfoot and gathered a lot of historical evidence about their sightings in Georgia.

Another researcher had posted a photo of a track found in Oglethorpe County on an online Bigfoot discussion board, and that was the first time that Pruitt had ever really met anyone interested in Sasquatch research in Georgia. He sent the man an email saying he had been researching Bigfoot in Georgia and was proud to find out that there was someone else doing research in the state. This changed his whole life, because the man got back in touch with him and explained how he conducted his research and about his affiliation with the BFRO. Pruitt had been a musician at that time, and when he found the BFRO, he really jumped "head first and body deep" into Bigfoot research. He decided that he wanted to make this a large part of his life. When he became affiliated with the BFRO, he had already done a great deal of research on Bigfoot, but he had not really done field research properly until he joined the organization.[19]

Pruitt focuses a lot of his energy on the Chattahoochee National Forest in the north Georgia mountains. On average, he spends from two thousand to twenty-five hundred hours a year in the woods tracking these creatures. Although he never goes out armed, he does take precautions, for he realizes that these animals are part of nature and should be respected as such. He believes that they are very curious about us, just as much as or more so than we are about them. Each time he goes on a lengthy outing in the woods, upon his return he gets asked if he saw any Sasquatch. His response is always the same: "I am sure that I was seen by a few Sasquatch." Pruitt believes that one of the reasons we have such difficulty finding Sasquatch is that they are hiding from humans. In fact, he suggests that they are not hiding from anything in the forest other than us. He feels that although they hide, they still watch us carefully as we wander into their territory. In fact, he tells the story of an encounter he had with the animals while camping with friends on property that had been in his family for many years.[20]

The encounter happened when he and his friends decided to camp on this family owned property that was completely surrounded by a national forest and located in a very remote area about an hour from where he grew up. On this occasion, he arrived at the cabin around ten-thirty in the evening. He was standing on the porch enjoying the air, when he heard something walking about fifty feet away in the woods. He was familiar with the area because as a child he had been there a lot with his family, and it was quite unusual to hear anything of this nature in that vicinity.

All of a sudden, he could hear the sounds of heavy footsteps near the cabin. One of the friends who was with him had also accompanied Pruitt to the cabin a lot and was familiar with the terrain. He too heard the noise and was startled. He came out on the porch and sat with Pruitt to listen. Shortly afterwards, Pruitt put on first-generation night vision viewers, although he confesses that they were of low quality. When another friend walked to the car to investigate noises coming from that vicinity, Pruitt decided to join him. At this point, it was decided that there were obviously two creatures near the cabin, as two sets of footsteps could be heard. As the boys approached the car, the footsteps stopped, but Pruitt was quick to point out that they did not hear the creatures walk away; they just stopped moving. The boys became frightened. After a while, they decided to go back into the cabin. One friend went upstairs to go to sleep, while the others built a fire in the fireplace and had to go outside to retrieve wood for the fire. Upon going outside, they heard the movement start again. This time, the footsteps seemed to be coming toward them.

Pruitt had been joined outside by a friend, and he mentioned that it appeared the animals were being tactical. Pruitt then decided to communicate with them. He tried some whooping calls and such, and then he tried holding his hands in the air as he spoke to the animals as if they were children. They never responded, but continued moving around very slowly with big, heavy steps. Pruitt could feel the tension mounting, but decided to challenge the animals. He picked up a piece of firewood and proceeded to throw it in the direction from which the sounds were coming. He did not want to hit the animals, only cause them to move around so they would be visible, or perhaps cause them to respond verbally. He attempted an overhand throw, and just as the wood went airborne, to his left came a sound as if a large hand had hit the tin roof of a nearby shed. When this happened, the creatures moved. All of this activity happened while the wood was still moving through the air.

Pruitt felt that the creature to his left had seen him throw the firewood and preempted him by making a commotion to distract the boys. Strangely enough, no more movement was heard, and the boys decided to go inside the cabin for the night. Thinking about the incident later, Pruitt felt that the Sasquatch had been hunting near the cabin when the boys arrived for the night. He thinks that this area has now been claimed by Sasquatch as a potential hunting ground. That night, Pruitt and his friends had the fortunate experience of stumbling upon them as they were conducting a hunt.[21]

In terms of the creature itself, Pruitt thinks that the species of Sasquatch living in Georgia is the same as the species found in the Pacific Northwest. As evidence for this, he focuses on the tracks found in the South in comparison to those found in the Pacific Northwest. They are quite consistent throughout, having the same morphology, thus indicating that all of them are bipedal creatures and are of the same species. Furthermore, from reports he has received from those who have seen and encountered the animals in both regions, as well as his own research in both regions (Pruitt moved to Seattle, Washington to do research in that area in 2008), he feels that the behavioral patterns of both sets of animals are the same. In addition, Pruitt does not think that the southeastern Bigfoot, which includes the Georgia Bigfoot, is smaller than the Bigfoot of the Pacific Northwest. Whatever difference exists between the creatures of the Pacific Northwest and the Southeastern United States simply results from the differences in those two terrains. But across the continent, Pruitt says that all Sasquatch are the same thing — an unclassified great ape.[22]

Going further in trying to identify the Georgia Bigfoot, Pruitt has offered even more theories. He believes that Sasquatch in general and specifically in Georgia is related to *Gigantopithecus*, an ancient apelike species that existed thousands of years ago.[23] According to Dr. Jeff Meldrum of Idaho State University, the author of *Sasquatch: Legend Meets Science*, "The Giant Ape was first discovered when, in the 1930s, paleontologist Ralph von Koenigswald began searching the apothecary shops of eastern China for 'dragon bones' used as curatives in traditional Chinese medicine. The dragon bones were the fossilized teeth and bones of ancient mammals. In Hong Kong he came upon a single gigantic lower molar tooth of an unknown ape, twice the size of a corresponding gorilla tooth. He named the species *Gigantopithecus blacki*."[24] Of all the apes that have ever lived, it is the largest. Its estimated weight was around seven hundred pounds, and it stood nearly ten feet tall. According to both Pruitt and scientists like Meldrum, there is a theory that these giant apes, which originated in Asia, somehow migrated across the Bering land bridge, called Beringia, between present-day Alaska and Siberia. Pruitt believes that *Gigantopithecus* was an East Asian ape that evolved and lived alongside humans of that era and developed a somewhat similar lifestyle to them. Pruitt theorizes that humans migrated across the Bering land bridge, so it is more than plausible that these apes did as well.[25] The theory that these apes moved across the land bridge between Asia and North America is supported by Dr. Meldrum. While he says most scientists agree that the land bridge would have been more like a frozen wasteland or windswept tundra, the fossil record does bear out that vegetation on the land bridge at points in the past, especially in the early to middle Miocene, would have supported the lifestyle of these great apes. In fact, he argues that there was a "…continuous temperate corridor of deciduous broadleaf and coniferous forests [that] extended from northeast Asia, across the land connection in the region of the present Bering Strait, down across western North America into the Pacific Northwest."[26]

Pruitt, having studied the theories of men like Meldrum and the evidence they use to support them, believes that while *Gigantopithecus* did end up in the forests of what would become the Pacific Northwest, it is not that great of a leap in logic to assume that these apes would then migrate to other parts of North America, including what is now called the southeastern United States. He believes the descendents of these animals are our present-day Sasquatch. The number one thing that convinces him of this is the size of the animals reported by eyewitnesses and the size of the tracks they leave. He says that according to leading scientists in the field, no other animal since that time has ever achieved the height of these apes. He feels that for people to describe for the past four hundred years an upright, hair-covered animal that is manlike in some respect, it just stands to reason that Sasquatch is related to *Gigantopithecus*. With this in mind, Pruitt calls modern-day Bigfoot great apes, much like *Gigantopithecus* was considered a great ape. He points to sightings by witnesses in Georgia and elsewhere indicating that Bigfoot has large arms that are about eighty percent as long as their legs, a characteristic they share with *Gigantopithecus*. Other features they share are their hair-covered bodies, bipedalism, and huge footprints. There is no doubt in his mind that these North American great apes, including the species found in Georgia, are descendents of *Gigantopithecus blacki*.[27]

Perhaps one of the most persistent questions that people have about Bigfoot research in Georgia and elsewhere is "Why has one never been caught?" Pruitt believes that this can be answered by looking at the behavioral patterns of Sasquatch's ancestor, Giganto. He says that Giganto, like the Sasquatch of today, had a way of avoiding humans, not because they simply wanted to, but because it was necessary for survival. Pruitt feels that these great apes were probably driven almost to extinction because of humans preying on them. This certainly changed the behavioral patterns of Giganto. They had to adapt to a new lifestyle to survive. Some of them obviously did. He feels that they would probably have had to become nocturnal, leaving no signs of life behind, moving around in small numbers, and being very sly and stealthy. This fits what Pruitt knows about Sasquatch today and he comments that this, more than anything, can answer why these creatures are so elusive and have avoided capture.[28]

One might also ask how these large creatures can survive in Georgia, especially in light of the growing population and decrease in the amount of lands untouched by man and his need for development and settlement. According to Pruitt, there is still more than enough space for these animals to live and hide in the state, specifically in areas like the Chattahoochee National Forest, a region where he conducts much of his research. In addition, he feels that the food supply in Georgia's wilderness can support the eating habits of the Georgia Bigfoot. Pruitt calls these animals "generalized" omnivores, meaning that they eat many different foods that are readily available in the wilds of the state. He mentions that there is a high population of deer in Georgia, and that deer are a main foodstuff in the Sasquatch diet. In addition, these animals do eat plants, and plant life is still quite abundant in Georgia's forests. Other than deer and plants, these animals are said to feed on wild pigs and fish. There is also evidence of Georgia Sasquatch foraging for food around farms in the fields of rural Georgia. He says that it should be noted that while they are good hunters, they also depend on gathering to support their population. Pruitt thinks that they really would not have a noticeable effect on the environment, no more than deer. The signs they leave behind are very scanty, in terms of feeding. They feed on some of the same food as bears and deer, also making it harder to distinguish where they have been and where they have hunted in the state. Many people mistake the byproducts of Sasquatch hunting and feeding patterns for those of bear and deer, thus making their feeding habits and diet a partial reason for their being hard to find.[29]

In the pages that follow, there are many reports of Bigfoot sightings all across the state of Georgia, from the north Georgia mountains to the central portion of the state and the Georgia Islands on the coast. One might wonder if these are all the same animals — in other words, does the Georgia Bigfoot migrate? Pruitt believes that they do not. Again, logic dictates this feeling. To begin, Pruitt feels that these animals would not be able to make such long treks. The possibility of being seen would be too great, especially for an animal that has evolved and survived because they remain aloof and out of sight of humans, their only natural enemies. Pruitt believes that they have what he calls "home turf and range." These are areas where family units live and hunt, areas where they feel safe and have been successful at surviving. In addition to running the risk of being discovered, there are other reasons they do not migrate, chief among them being that they might fall into areas where they would not be able to find enough food or run into large concentrations of other predatory animals that might compete with them for game and food sources. Also, moving around a good bit might bring them to areas where they would come in contact with more humans. Pruitt believes that these animals have adapted so well that they have learned the areas where humans travel and congregate, and they avoid these areas. He says that they have evolved and adapted by understanding that it is better and safer to remain on their "home turf" so that they can easily locate food and water.[30]

In addition to Matt Pruitt, there are other Georgians out there who have staked their reputation on the existence of the Georgia Bigfoot. One is a trained paramedic who spent six years as part of the United States Army Reserves, half of that time with the 11th Special Forces Group. He studied sports medicine at the University of Georgia, and in 1994 became an EMT. Also, he has done extensive studies in herpetology, specifically in the area of venomous snakes. He developed and manages one of the largest websites on venomous snakes. Medical doctors, professors, and even the Arizona Poison Control center have all recognized this former Army Ranger for his expertise and his research on poisonous snakes.

However, because of the sensitive nature of his work, he chose not to reveal his name in this publication. I will refer to him as Ranger.

Ranger has conducted a great deal of Sasquatch research in Georgia. He has been associated with the Bigfoot Field Researchers Organization, a Sasquatch research organization that will be discussed later in this book, and also worked with a team of other researchers in Georgia, including Matt Pruitt. Ranger feels that many of the Sasquatch in Georgia can be found in the North Georgia area, specifically in the mountains. He believes that the area provides better mobility for the creatures and that development like what can be found in the metro-Atlanta area has interfered with the foot travel of these animals. Development in central Georgia, including Macon, has also interfered with the habits of Sasquatch living in that specific area. In terms of what type of places in the state make good homes for these animals, Ranger feels that forests with planted pines or any which are man-made do not provide the best habitats for Sasquatch. These animals, according to Ranger, dwell best in heavy-growth forests, like those national forests that have been set aside as public lands. In addition, river basins provide a good habitat, and, in Ranger's opinion, these animals are drawn to river basins because they are usually not traveled a lot by humans, especially late at night.[31]

One of the most common questions that people have when it comes to Bigfoot, other than whether or not they exist, is if these animals pose any threat to the human population. Both Pruitt and Ranger agree that they do not. Pruitt feels that if they were a threat, people would be more aware of them and would discuss them a lot more. He likes to refer to comments from Matthew Moneymaker, head of the Bigfoot Field Researchers Organization. According to Moneymaker, people usually talk about Great White sharks in the context of them attacking humans, and people are very aware of Great White sharks because of this. This is not so with Sasquatch.

Pruitt also thinks that we should remember that these animals are very fearful of us. At the same time, he says, they are curious about us, although in a face-to-face encounter we would feel more threatened than they would. Pruitt says that these animals do approach humans in houses, tents, and cars more than likely due to their curiosity. In addition, he says that these animals would do things to intimidate humans and get them to leave areas that the animals customarily use for hunting, because with humans there, the hunting would be next to impossible. This kind of interaction would be more commonly associated with a Sasquatch encounter than with an attack.[32] Ranger tends to agree with Pruitt's assessment. According to him, "These animals generally just try to scare the heck out of people to get them out of their area." Ranger cites a sighting in White County, Georgia, where a Sasquatch threw a huge log in the road. When the witness turned around to see what had happened, he spotted the creature and remarked that it appeared to have rage in its face. Ranger feels that the witness had strayed into the animal's habitat, or perhaps there was an infant or wounded Sasquatch in the area.[33]

Ranger does mention that there are some instances where Bigfoot has attacked humans; indeed, there are reports of some having lured children to them and picked them up, and other times they were only seen pointing or motioning to them. However, most of these reports have come from outside Georgia. Philip Rife, in his book *Bigfoot across America*, writes about an incident in Lincoln County, Tennessee, where a Bigfoot attempted to "snatch a four-year-old boy from his yard... His mother heard him scream, and rushed outside just in time to grab him and carry him inside the house."[34]

Matt Pruitt hypothesizes that it is possible that Sasquatch children may look a little like human infants. It is true that chimp and ape babies do bear a similarity to human babies, so perhaps Sasquatch is attracted to human children because there might be a resemblance to their children. Pruitt adds, however, that this is pure speculation.[35] Although no aggression was shown toward children, there are reports of Sasquatch in Georgia doing harm to adult humans, specifically the Okefenokee incident in 1829 and the August 1955 incident at Kinchafoonee Creek. Those encounters will be discussed in more detail in the chapter on sightings from Georgia history.

If one wonders if Sasquatch could potentially be harmful to humans, then it would stand to reason that there would be questions about how many of these creatures live in Georgia. When asked this question, Matt Pruitt responded, "I don't know, and I am not sure that anyone could ever know." Pruitt says that the amount of time it would take to locate all family groups would allow for birth and death of the species, further skewing the numbers. In addition, he says that it is almost impossible to find, follow, and track these animals, so there is no way of telling. He does offer an educated guess of one hundred, but says that this is absolutely nothing more than pure speculation. He does feel that the greatest concentration of these animals would be in the North Georgia Mountains around White, Rabun, Lumpkin, Gilmer, and Fannin counties. If this seems like a wide expanse, it is. He says that these animals are rare and do not live in every forest. They live in small numbers and indeed are spread out just enough to keep a viable breeding population. Pruitt feels that the population of these animals in the state should be gauged by how many live per square mile. He thinks that they do have to come in contact with other family groups to mate, and this process could take many years. In fact, he says that it may take a Sasquatch up to ten years to find a mate. Pruitt says, "It is impossible to give any reasonable estimate of their population. I don't know if we will ever know exactly how many of them there are. I do know they live in small numbers and are very rare. Their numbers are high enough to have a breeding population."[36]

Research to find the elusive creature continues in the state. As people like Pruitt tromp through the woods and look for evidence that the giants have walked that way, they are prodded on by the many reports that continue to come in from eyewitnesses around the state who claim to have seen the creature. Modern sightings are common, but Bigfoot sightings are not exclusively modern. As history shows, sightings of these creatures go back centuries in Georgia. In fact, the first inhabitants of Georgia told stories that lead many to believe they lived alongside these elusive creatures. In addition to that, stories and folktales told by early white settlers in the state indicate that these animals had a significant presence.

2
Indian Legends and Other Stories

Long before European settlers came to Georgia shores, native tribes dotted the landscape. While there are numbers of local tribes such as the Coweta, Yamacraw, and others, the two main tribes of Georgia on which this chapter will focus are the Cherokees and Creeks. While most scholars would argue that there are really no legends of either tribe that specifically deal with what we would call Bigfoot, the debate is far from over. Others who have been studying these animals for generations look at their stories about giants and animals and see evidence of Bigfoot encounters and characteristics of these creatures. While modern sightings are plentiful and there is much evidence out there indicating that European settlers who came to Georgia had encounters with these animals, the stories of the Native Americans in Georgia are quite interesting and stir debate among those in the Bigfoot research community. Before looking at some of those legends, as well as stories told by early settlers, it is important to take a brief look at the history of these two major tribes in the state.

The Cherokee Indians once occupied the northern region of the state. According to James Mooney in his book *Myths of the Cherokee*, the tribe once held the entire Allegheny region from the headstreams of the Kanawha and the Tennessee Rivers southward almost to the present-day city of Atlanta, Georgia. The Cherokee lands also ran from the Blue Ridge on the east to the Cumberland on the west, an area of almost forty thousand square miles. Their territory included the states of Virginia, Tennessee, North Carolina, South Carolina, Georgia, and Alabama. Mooney also points out that there were no fixed boundaries in Cherokee territory; their frontiers were challenged on almost all fronts by rival tribes who also claimed the area.

By the time the Spanish arrived, the Cherokee were already established in the mountains of Georgia. The first Spanish explorer to penetrate their territory was De Soto, although there was little interaction at all with the tribe there. In 1654, the English first made contact with the Cherokee in Virginia. In addition, Mooney also reports that during much of the 1700s, the Cherokee were engaged in warfare with their neighbors. Among these wars were ones with the Creeks for control of upper Georgia. In 1718, there was a planned attack by the Cherokees on the Creek town of Coweta. The attack never happened because of the presence of English, Spanish, and French traders in the area who were attempting to negotiate peaceful relations with the Cherokee. The Creeks, while comfortable working with the English and other Europeans, still carried their hatred for the Cherokee and pledged renewed attacks.

Perhaps one of the most important battles between the two tribes happened at Tali'wa in the year 1755.[37]

The Creeks also had an interesting history in Georgia. The Creeks were the first Native Americans with which the founder of Georgia, James Oglethorpe, came in contact — specifically the Yamacraw and their chief, Tomochichi. The Creeks did not have an old political identity in the New World when the English arrived; moreover, they were not a nation when Columbus arrived in 1492. Most of the natives of the southeastern portion of what would become the United States lived in what historians call mound-building societies. After about 1400 AD, these natives organized themselves into small chiefdoms and spread out along Georgia's river valleys. Although the introduction of disease by European settlers almost dealt these native populations a death blow, they recovered around the late 1600s. It was after this time that they began to build more complex political alliances, and by 1715 some were calling these allied groups "Creeks," which was the short version for "Indians living on Ochese Creek." Ochese Creek is near Macon, but European traders soon began to refer to all of the natives in the Deep South as "Creeks," thus the name stuck and remains in use today.[38]

As more and more Europeans began to settle in Georgia, they started to trade slaves and deerskins with the Creeks. This trade encouraged closer cultural ties between the two groups. Some European men even married Creek women. Some of their children, like Alexander McGillivray and William McIntosh, became famous Creek leaders. Over time, the state of Georgia began to see the Creeks as an obstacle to the plantation system and slaveholding social structure that was the backbone of the economy. As a result, the government of Georgia backed by their allies in the federal government began to put pressure on the

Creeks to cede their land. The Treaty of New York in 1790, Fort Wilkinson in 1802, and Washington in 1805, were all the products of this pressure. Although these treaties resulted in the acquisition of much Creek land, the final straw did not come until the Treaty of Indian Springs in 1824 and the Treaty of Washington in 1825. It was these final agreements that secured all remaining Creek land in Georgia. The Creeks were then forced to move to the Oklahoma Territory to begin a new life, hundreds of miles away from their native lands.[39]

Indeed, the Creeks were the Native Americans who occupied most of the territory in Georgia. The Cherokees lived in what is the extreme northern part of the state, mainly in the mountainous region. As such, it might stand to reason that the Creeks would have a multitude of stories and tales to tell about Bigfoot, since they occupied most of the ground in the state, but that would not be a safe bet. Research bears out that there are not many Creek legends at all that reflect Bigfoot. In fact, Sam Riley, in his article "A Search for the Cultural Bigfoot: Folklore or Fakelore?" suggests that there was only one Creek legend that sounded remotely like Bigfoot, and that the legend only originated after the tribe was removed from Georgia and placed on Indian land in the West. What he refers to is the legend of Este Chupco, which translates as "tall person." The creature was never seen, but could be heard tromping through the forests slapping trees.[40] That the legend of Este Chupco is a Creek legend perpetuated only after the removal of the Creeks to the West is backed by the famous Creek Indian writer, journalist, and poet, Alex Posey, who lived in Oklahoma and was born in Eufaula, Oklahoma on August 3, 1873. In the book, *Alex Posey: Creek Poet, Journalist, and Humorist* by Daniel Littlefield, Posey's writings about the legend of Este Chupco can be found. Posey claimed that they were wood spirits who lived in the nearby

Tulledega Hills.[41] Taken at face value, it would appear that Este Chupco was a legend born in the Sooner State, not the Peach State. However, it is not quite that simple.

The legend seems to have roots in the Southeast. On the episode entitled "Swamp Beast," part of the popular History Channel series *Monster Quest*, Jay McGirt of the Creek-Seminole Nation is interviewed. In his remarks he says, "Our elders say that they are to be respected, and that they are to live in peace." McGirt is referring to the legend of Este Chupco, for he mentions right before these remarks that the swamp beasts are called Este Chupco in his native language. He goes on to say that the Creeks and Seminoles have never felt that it was important to try to locate or capture Este Chupco, for they are to be left alone and have never bothered anyone.

This episode is dedicated to the search for the Swamp Beast that is said to roam the swamps and lowlands of Florida, Georgia, Louisiana, and Texas. The episode clearly focuses on the deeper portion of the Southeast, not Oklahoma or the Plains.[42] Perhaps Este Chupco was a legend that was taken with the Creeks from Georgia and Alabama upon their removal from those areas in the 1830s. Nevertheless, Sam Riley was correct in asserting that the Creeks did not have many legends that seemed in reference to Bigfoot, but it is not so clear that Este Chupco does not point to Bigfoot, and taking into consideration the argument above, it is not so clear that Este Chupco is a Creek story born or reflecting the Creek's time in Oklahoma after they were removed from Georgia. In addition, there are Bigfoot researchers who argue that Este Chupco's activity of "slapping the trees" sounds a good bit like the common Bigfoot behavior of "wood-knocking." The evidence and points do merit debate.

Turning to the legends of the Cherokees, we find quite a bit of material for debate and discussion. The first and foremost legend that gets the attention of Bigfoot researchers is that of the Judaculla, oftentimes spelled Jutaculla, or as reflected in James Mooney's work, *Myths of the Cherokee,* Tsul'Kalu. According to the legend, Tsul'Kalu is also called the slant-eyed giant. He comes to visit a young girl who lived near the Pigeon River with her mother. Having received counsel from her mother to choose a good hunter for a husband, the girl commenced to await the arrival of her beau, who hopefully would have good hunting skills. She slept outside, and one night, a tall stranger came to her and asked to court her. Professing to be a great hunter, the stranger stayed the entire night, but upon morning's first light, he declared that he would have to return to his home. As a gift, he left her a deer to share with her mother, but the young girl had not seen the stranger's face. He returned again the next night, and as before, he left before daylight and bestowed upon his love a gift of meat — only this time, it was two deer carcasses. The mother and daughter were grateful, but the mother spoke the wish that her daughter's new sweetheart would bring them some wood. The legend mentions that the stranger could hear their thoughts, and so the next day, in response to what the mother had said, he brought several trees and placed them near their door, branches, roots, and all. Basically, the reading of the legend seems to indicate that the stranger uprooted the trees and carried them to his new love's door. However, when the girl's mother complained that he had not chopped the wood, the stranger discontinued bringing wood from the forest.[43]

After a while, the girl's mother began to request a visit with her new love. When the girl reported this to Tsul'Kalu, he declined, commenting that if her mother saw his face, she would be frightened. However, the girl persisted, and finally, the giant agreed to allow her mother to see him, but warned that her mother must not comment on his frightening looks.

The next morning, instead of leaving, as he was accustomed, he stayed and allowed the mother to see him. As feared, the mother was frightened and ran away crying. The giant was furious and left to return to his own country, declaring that he would never allow her mother to look upon his face again. Shortly afterwards, the girl began her monthly cycle and her mother disposed of the blood by throwing it in the river, which brought the giant back to visit the girl once he had found it. He subsequently found the worm that would lead to the birth of a child belonging to him and the girl. Angry at the disrespect he felt he and his child were being shown by the girl's mother, he told the girl to leave her mother and return with him to his own country where she would live with him and his people. The girl did.

In a short time, the girl's brother came for a visit, at which time his mother, stricken with grief and loneliness over the girl's departure, asked her son to bring his sister back. He agreed, and followed their tracks. He even commented that it was easy to follow these tracks, for the stranger's were gigantic. He came close to where the race of giants lived near a place called Tsunegun'yi. He could hear a sound like the beating of drums. Upon arrival, he saw his sister there dancing among her husband's people. He visited with his sister and even returned there a few times. Like his mother, he became curious as to what his sister's husband looked like, for each time he came to visit her, she came out to meet him and never allowed him to see her new husband. When he requested to see him, Tsul'Kalu asked him to return in new dress and go home to tell his people to fast for seven days. The people of his village were eager to comply, for they wanted to see Tsul'Kalu, who they say, "... owned all the game in the mountains." The story ends with a stranger breaking the fast and Tsul'Kalu denying the brother the privilege of seeing him face to face.[44]

Bigfoot researchers find a lot in that story to talk about. According to Matt Pruitt, there is much to be discussed in the name Slant-Eyed Giant, another name by which Jutaculla is known. Pruitt says a rough interpretation of what it means to be slanting or sloping could be a tapering and sloping forehead like that of Sasquatch. The main point is the size of the giant in the story and the fact that the Cherokees called him lord of the woods. The fact that he is a giant figure is also important. He is not a giant of the sort we would find in *Gulliver's Travels*, but is a giant in terms of size alone.[45]

In the legend, the giant returns to his own country, and in one part, the legend says he went off in the direction of Tsunegun'yi. Supposedly, this is the place where Tsul'Kalu lived. Examining the history of this place, one would find out that Tsunegun'yi, according to James Mooney, is located at "... Tennessee Bald, in North Carolina, where the Haywood, Jackson, and Transylvania county lines come together, on the ridge separating the waters of Pigeon River from those flowing into Tennessee Creek and Cany Fork of the Tuckasegee, southeastward from Waynesville and Webster." Mooney goes on to write that the name may mean "at the white place" and possibly refers to a bald spot of about one hundred acres atop the mountain. Whites called this Jutaculla old fields, a name that obviously came from the Cherokee legend that the bald was a clearing made by Jutaculla for a farm. Nearby is Jutaculla Rock, a rock covered with petroglyphs said to have been made when the giant jumped from his farm at the bald spot into the creek below. Mooney also mentions that other researchers have found that this area was also called "Old Field Mountain," and that some pioneers in the area recalled that the native Cherokees there claimed that it was home to the Indian Satan.[46]

In addition to Jutaculla Rock, there is another place near this area that also has a stone where prints can still be seen. According to Mooney, "Shining Rock or Cold Mountain, between the Forks of Pigeon River in Haywood county, North Carolina, is known to the Cherokee as Datsu'nalasgun-yi, 'where their tracks are this way,' on account of a rock at its base, toward Sonoma and three miles south of the trail, upon which are impressions said to be the footprints made by the giant and his children on their way to Tsunegun-yi." Mooney also mentions that famed Tennessee historian John Haywood lumped this rock and its stories with that of Track Rock Gap in Blairsville, Georgia.[47] Haywood is famous for his histories of Tennessee, and Haywood County in Tennessee is named in his memory.[48]

So what is Track Rock Gap? Mooney describes it as a gap about five miles east of the settlement of Blairsville in what is Union County, Georgia. There are numbers of soapstone rocks on a trail through the gap and these rocks are covered with petroglyphs. Mooney recalls that the Cherokee called this place Datsu'nalasgun-yi, as they did Shining Rock between the forks of Pigeon River in Haywood County, North Carolina. Mooney also mentions that the Cherokee give another meaning to this word — "Where there are tracks."[49] While this is a little different from the meaning above given for the location in North Carolina, it is basically the same idea and just a slightly different translation. Once again, Tennessee historian John Haywood associates this place, as well as the one in Haywood County, North Carolina, with the legend of Tsul'Kalu.

Matt Pruitt is of the opinion that Track Rock Gap is a place where Indians recorded their experience with Sasquatch. Pruitt mentions that natives had the habit of recording what they saw around them, an explanation for petroglyphs and rock drawings in Indian territories, and that the drawings at Track Rock Gap are no exception. Pruitt feels that Track Rock Gap and its markings are simply native peoples' historical records and their observations of Sasquatch in the area.[50] If indeed this is true, then perhaps Tsul'Kalu (Jutaculla/Judaculla) is more than a legend; perhaps it was an attempt of Cherokee Indians to rationalize what they saw and the existence of Sasquatch. Perhaps Tsul'Kalu was a Sasquatch, or more than one. The rocks mentioned above would then be more than just part of a legend — they would be ancient historical markers.

In addition to these places, Matt Pruitt says that there is other evidence that native tribes in Georgia have had contact with Sasquatch. He points to Blood Mountain for that evidence. Located in Union County, Georgia, not far from Blairsville, Blood Mountain was the site of a battle between Cherokee and Creek Indian tribes for control of territory. The Cherokees won the battle, which was fought at Slaughter Gap between Blood Mountain and Slaughter Mountain. Both Slaughter Gap and Slaughter Mountain are called so due to the tragic fight between the two tribes. A visit to the area will reveal a Georgia historical marker that includes the following inscription:

Blood Mountain, elevation 4458 ft. Chattahoochee National Forest. In Cherokee mythology the mountain was one of the homes of the Nunnehi or Immortals, the "People Who Live

Anywhere," a race of Spirit People who lived in great townhouses in the highlands of the old Cherokee Country. One of these mythical townhouses stood near Lake Trahlyta. As a friendly people, they often brought lost hunters and wanderers to their townhouses for rest and care before guiding them back to their homes. Before the coming of white settlers, the Creeks and Cherokees fought a disastrous and bloody battle in Slaughter Gap between Slaughter and Blood Mountains.[51]

Pruitt contends that Blood Mountain is also the source of quite a few reported Sasquatch sightings. As a field researcher with the BFRO, Pruitt has followed up on several reports from the area and says that his files contain sightings from there. Additional legends associated with Blood Mountain include a race of people who can be heard drumming. Pruitt says that this is more than likely the wood-knocking so common to Sasquatch. Pruitt says that since wood-knocking is used as a communication tool among these animals to keep track of one another when they spread out foraging for food, the animals are probably doing this as they hunt on the mountain, a prime location for food due to its abundance of plant and animal life. The drumming that natives and other peoples have heard there was probably Sasquatch wood-knocking. Pruitt mentions that his research on the legend of the drumming people of Blood Mountain indicates that their drumming happens at night. To him, this also fits neatly into the characteristics of Sasquatch, as they are known to forage for food under cover of nighttime darkness to avoid contact with humans. So to Pruitt, Blood Mountain is just another piece of evidence for the existence of Sasquatch in Georgia.[52]

Researching the history of Native American tribes in Georgia is a difficult task due to the fact that many tribes did not keep written records. Their traditions and histories were passed down orally in many instances, and their legends and folklore were passed down the same way. If it were not for the work of James Mooney, Cherokee myth and legend might have been even more difficult to understand and study than it is today. The Creeks present challenges even greater than the Cherokees in this respect. However, the legends of Tsul'Kalu provide us with a topic for much debate. There is also room to debate the legend of Este Chupco among the Creeks. Were these legends based on Cherokee and Creek interactions with Sasquatch in the southeastern United States, including Georgia? Bigfoot researchers like Matt Pruitt believe they were. Places like Track Rock Gap, Blood Mountain, and Slaughter Mountain may stand as markers to their existence, just like the historical and modern sightings often do. There are many uncertainties in this portion of Georgia history, but what is certain is that when European settlers came to Georgia, they spread out across the landscape, and, as they did, they saw things in the woods of Georgia that they could not explain. As the next chapter shows, some of those sightings could have been of the legendary creature.

3
Encounters from History

After James Oglethorpe and the first settlers landed at Yamacraw Bluff on the Savannah River in 1733, white settlers began to explore and then later put down roots along the Georgia coast. This trend continued, and by 1750, Georgians were petitioning strongly for the admission of slavery in Georgia, an institution that had been banned by Oglethorpe and the Trustees. Georgians were demanding the introduction of this "peculiar institution" because Georgia land had proven to be quite fertile. One crop in particular grew very well in Georgia — cotton. The growth of cotton plantations and production in Georgia was forever cemented in the state with the invention of the cotton gin by Eli Whitney in 1791. Cotton production soared, and by 1801, the state was producing twenty thousand bales per year, up from only one thousand in 1791, when

Whitney invented the contraption that made the ginning of cotton quite easy.

As Georgians began to push into the unsettled wilderness away from the coastal region, they encountered Native American tribes not so willing to give up their lands. As history suggests, that did not stop Americans who were hard-pressed for farmland to make their dream of owning land and reaping a bountiful harvest in the new nation a reality. Treaties with Native American tribes, as underhanded as they appeared, opened up more land to white settlement. As pressure from the commercial sector mounted, the state government continued to push native tribes farther and farther out of their original territory in Georgia. The eviction started with the Choctaw in 1831 and continued with the Seminoles in 1832, The Creek in 1834, and the Chickasaw in 1837, ultimately culminating in the removal of all Cherokees from North Georgia in 1838 on what has been deemed the notorious Trail of Tears.[53] This now meant the entire state was open for white settlement, and within a few years, the population of Georgia began to grow.

Due to population growth, Georgians would soon be in almost all corners of the state. While there are vast tracts of land in Georgia that are still unsettled — for example, the Chattahoochee National Forest in the north Georgia mountains — almost every corner of the state has seen considerable growth since the post-Revolutionary period. As can be expected, this growth and movement of white settlers displaced animal life in those areas. It had already taken its toll on the Native American population, as evidenced by their removal from the state. Animals, on the other hand, were not herded and moved along a trail to be relocated on land in the West; they would have to make adjustments where they were. Without a doubt, this new surge in population would affect the alleged creature called Bigfoot like any other animal in the woods. Sightings going all the way back to the early 1800s in Georgia suggest that if this creature exists, it was making its presence known as more and more white settlers began to wander into its territory. What follows are selected reports from the 1800s through the late 1980s. Of course there are others, but these are some of the more interesting ones.

One of the earliest sightings on record in Georgia happened in the Georgia mountains, specifically in Rabun County, although no year was given for the original sighting. A group of hunters exploring the area encountered an animal with a strange appearance. There are some similarities to modern Bigfoot sightings, especially the height and the presence of hair. The surveyors claimed that the animal was eight feet tall, with bluish hair and big ears like a jackass. While Bigfoot sighting reports rarely mention long ears, the height and presence of bluish hair does seem to bear some similarity to Bigfoot/Sasquatch. The explorers must either have yelled or shot at it, for they mentioned that the animal was apparently deaf. In 1816, a group of land surveyors from Virginia returned to the area along with others in an attempt to capture the animal, but they were unsuccessful and the creature remained at large in the hills of Rabun County.[54]

Another encounter took place in the Okefenokee Swamp, located in the southeast corner of the state along the Florida border. Although the actual encounter happened on the Florida side of the swamp and is also a part of the Florida Swamp Ape legend, the alleged beast had been seen all over the area in both Georgia's and Florida's part of the Okefenokee. The encounter is perhaps one of the most talked-about stories in southern Bigfoot lore and is one of the most hair-raising.

The story first appeared in a Milledgeville, Georgia, newspaper and concerned two men and a young boy who journeyed into the Okefenokee in 1829 to investigate Creek Indian legends about a race of giants who lived in the swamp. Legend has it that the Creeks built low earthen mounds in the swamp where they buried their honored dead.

To investigate what became the legend of the "Man Mountain," the men and the boy journeyed into the deep interior of the swamp. After a journey of two weeks, they came upon a footprint that was eighteen inches long and nine inches wide. Thinking back to the Creek Indian legend about giants in the swamp, they decided to suspend their search. Returning home, they discussed what they had seen with locals, and eventually their story reached hunters nearby. These hunters, all from Florida and nine in total, decided to do some investigative work for themselves. They ventured into the swamp in search of the giant. After seeing what they thought to be the giant's tracks, they proceeded further into the interior of the Okefenokee. After a few days, they were setting up camp to settle in for the night when a couple of the hunters fired off their rifles to kill a wild animal that was descending upon them. The sound of their rifles obviously startled the creature of which they were in pursuit, and shortly thereafter, he came upon their camp in full view of the hunting party. The group banded together, fired their rifles at the beast, and tried to defend themselves. Before killing the creature, five of the hunters were decapitated by it. The animal finally fell, and while it was lying on the ground, wallowing and writhing in pain, the four remaining hunters examined it. They found it to be around thirteen feet tall. In addition, they found his breadth and volume to be of "just proportions."[55] This story has survived the ages, and has become so much a part of Bigfoot and Swamp Ape legend that as part of its popular series *Monster Quest*, the History Channel reported the story during its broadcast about its investigation into the Florida Swamp Ape story. Although the finer details as described by wildlife biologist Tony Gerard were slightly different, the story was quite similar to ones reported by newspapers that carried the story in the early nineteenth century.[56]

The same swamp was part of a more recent story, too. One of the burial places in the swamp was on an island called Chesser Island, which is named for the family who owned it. Jim Miles, in his book *Weird Georgia*, reports that, in 1969, Tom Chesser told the *Atlanta Journal-Constitution Sunday Magazine* that in the 1920s he unearthed thirteen skeletons for a university professor who had hired him to excavate the mounds. According to Chesser, "Some of the skeletons were crossed... one on top of the other. Some were face-down. All of them were perfect when they were first discovered. Teeth even still had some glaze on them, but when air struck, it crumbled them. They were giants. Those jawbones would go over my whole face."[57]

Moving back to the 1800s, in 1883 the *New York Times* was the journal in which an episode involving what they called a "wild man" was reported. According to the popular northeastern paper, for some time a "wild man" had been generating some excitement along the lines of the Western and Atlantic Railroad, the very railroad from which the city of Atlanta got its name. According to the report, the "wild man" had been seen in the Morganville area along the lines of the railroad eating dead animals and was clothed in what looked like horsehide. On one particular morning, it was seen vigorously chewing on a dead rabbit it had in its hands. At one point, area citizens attempted to lasso the "wild man," but to no avail. As they drew closer to it, it made its escape and eluded them. The report claimed that it refused to talk and would disappear quickly into the woods.[58] Although it is not one hundred percent certain that what the residents of Morganville were seeing was a Bigfoot, there are several characteristics in this report that do match those commonly associated with tales of the creature elsewhere. First, it was eating dead animals, more specifically mentioned in the article as a rabbit. Rabbits are said to be a common staple in the Georgia Bigfoot's diet, and the consumption of dead animals is not something commonly associated with humans, even those that are feral — that is, unless the human has been totally raised in the wilds and has built a mighty strong tolerance to the bacteria and other problems associated with eating uncooked meat. Second, the report indicated that the "wild man" would not speak. Was this was because he could not, or was unable to communicate as a human because it was indeed not human? Third, the report indicated that this "wild man" was clothed in horsehide. Could this possibly be a misidentification, and that the horsehide covering was actually brown or black fur? These are questions worth pondering.

Not long afterwards, the Ridge and Valley region of Georgia was the home of another "wild man" that could have been the creature known as Bigfoot. Near Lookout Mountain in Walker County in the northwest corner of the state, a "wild man" was seen by a "reliable gentleman" who happened to be standing one hundred yards away, according to a report in the February 4, 1889, edition of the *Atlanta Constitution*. According to the report, the creature stood erect and shook his fist at the man, who described what he saw as 7 to 7½ feet tall. The man also mentioned that the animal was hairy like a bear and looked like it weighed around four hundred pounds. While standing near it, the man saw it throw a heavy stone toward him, at which time the man left the area in a hurry, ending up at a local business which the article called Frank Carter's shop. While there, the man told his story to a crowd of locals, who began a search of Lookout Mountain for the animal/creature.[59] A month later, the *Atlanta Constitution* reported another group of sightings of the "Wild Man" of Lookout Mountain. This time, his hair and beard were reported to be flowing to his waist, and he was said to have had fingernails and toenails that were long, so long indeed that they made his hands appear to be claws. He was said to have worn a trunk of bearskin with a bearskin robe thrown over his shoulder.[60]

It seems that the "wild man" returned once again to the pages of the *New York Times*, for on February 8, 1889, the paper reported that the citizens of Walker County, not far from Chattanooga, were again plagued by the appearance of a "wild man" tromping through the mountainous region of the county. According to the report, the citizens were getting quite excited over the possibility of the existence of a genuine wild man, who, as they report, was of "gigantic stature, covered with a thick growth of hair, and carries in his hand a huge knotted stick." The report further indicated that residents felt this "wild man" might be the "twin brother of Barnum's Wild Man, and [was] fierce and untamable." It appears that one man had an encounter with the creature and from a safe distance attempted to strike up a conversation with it. Apparently, this being did not seem interested in good old-fashioned southern conversation, as it began to shower the man with stones. At such a turn of events, the man who tried speaking to it decided that it would be the better part of wisdom to leave the area before encountering any more of the "wild man's" wrath.[61]

Another report comes from the Fayette County and Fulton County areas in the 1800s, although the specific date is not given. According to the report, two spinster sisters who lived in the area and whose last name was Comference reported that, one night, an animal of sorts ran under their house and started screaming like a woman. In its attempts to stand up under their home, it hit the underside of the house so hard that it buckled the wooden planks of the floor. Finally, the animal found its way out from under the house and ran off into the woods. The next day, the two sisters told their story to the neighbors, and the story became known as the legend of the "Comference Booger."[62]

Perhaps one of the strangest reports from the 1800s comes not from a Georgia newspaper, but from one in Louisiana. According to the *Lafayette Advertiser* of Lafayette, Louisiana, in 1887, one of the largest planters, a Mr. J. K. Beal of Jones County, Georgia, realized that railings from one of his fences were going missing. Whomever or whatever was taking the rails would take only the best, leaving behind those that were decaying and defective. As this continued to happen for some time, Beal noticed that his pigs were beginning to disappear as well. Nearby, he also noticed that someone or something had been taking corn from his cornfield. Soon, a party was organized to follow the trail left by the person who appeared to be taking the railings, swine, and corn. The party reached an area that towered above the landscape like a hill. It was there that they discovered a pen as large as a great house. The pen had been built of the stolen fences, and in the pen were the stolen pigs. In every direction, there were giant bear tracks. Inside the pen were also remains of the ears of corn that had been stolen from Beal's cornfields. Amazed at what they saw, the only explanation they could devise was that a bear was living in the woods, stealing the pigs and fencing, and was raising the animals on the corn for consumption during the winter.[63] While the theory is plausible in many respects, one thing derails it — bears cannot build pens and do not usually steal animals for raising and later consumption; rather, they capture them and eat them on site. This behavior is more in line with that of Bigfoot. Bears are not capable of such high-order planning and preparation.

In Greene County not far from Athens, Georgia, there was a mysterious creature that walked the streets of Greensboro between midnight and one AM many mornings. According to a report in the *Herald-Journal* on October 4, 1901, the "spook," as the paper referred to it, had been named "Walking Bet." The being was described as seven to eight feet tall and wearing a black dress and heavy veil. It would walk the streets in the early morning hours and disappear without anyone having the courage to approach and investigate.[64] The black dress and heavy veil could very well have been the black fur, which usually covers the body of animals reported as Bigfoot, and the heavy veil could have been the deep-black skin that these animals are said to have on their faces. The creature was described as seven to eight feet tall, which is the height most often reported in Georgia Bigfoot sightings. Although no one ever identified "Walking Bet," the description matches many reports of Bigfoot across Georgia, and as later chapters will show, Greene County and nearby Clarke County are home to many Bigfoot sightings in the twentieth century.

A few years after the episode of Walking Bet, Worth County, Georgia, was haunted by what the *Atlanta Constitution* called a "mysterious beast." Near the community of Bridgeboro in southwestern Worth County, a farmer reported that a wild beast had raided his farm, killing a half-grown calf and taking it into the woods, where it proceeded to devour the animal. A few days later, the beast appeared in another area of the county and killed a farmer's half-grown pigs and sheep. The report indicated that women and children were afraid to come outside for fear of being attacked by the beast. One observer, traveling through the woods late one evening, saw the beast and reported that it was large, possibly a young male, and appeared to be able to jump a fence with a full-grown cow in its mouth. Perhaps the last part is a bit of an exaggeration, but residents were alarmed at the manner in which they found the remains of animals it had attacked and eaten, mostly leaving the half-devoured carcasses in the woods.[65] Some residents felt that the animal was a wolf, but the earlier descriptions of it as a young male able to jump a fence with a full-grown cow in its mouth lead one to believe that the animal might have been much bigger than a wolf. While some may speculate that it was a bear, eyewitnesses would more than likely have easily identified the animal as such, and the report would have reflected as much. Once again, there is no hundred-percent degree of certainty, and the report seems quite mysterious.

In the 1950s in Troup County, a county that sits on the Georgia and Alabama border, a young farm boy was attempting to feed his family hogs when he saw a Bigfoot creature. The boy estimated that the animal stood around eight feet tall and that it weighed around four or five hundred pounds. The animal he saw had brownish hair that hung all over its body, and shortly after the sighting, four-toed footprints were found near the hog pen in question.[66]

In 1951 near Boston, Georgia in Thomas County, which sits on the Florida border, a woman reported that she and her husband decided to go outside to investigate what was causing the family dogs to bark uncontrollably. Once outside, they saw what they thought was a giant man covered in dark hair. The dogs had the animal cornered on one side of the porch. The husband shot at the animal, causing it to run off into the woods. The woman also reported that her uncle had discovered twenty-inch footprints outside his cabin after seeing what he thought was an African-American male peering at him through the window of his cabin. The fact that the uncle mistook what he saw for an African-American man attests to the fact that the animal was covered with black hair, giving it a darker appearance. Upon seeing the intruder, the uncle went outside and shot at it with his pistol, causing it to run off hurriedly into the woods.[67]

While most encounters with what witnesses call Bigfoot in Georgia have not been violent, on August 1, 1955, in southwest Georgia near Kinchafoonee Creek, which runs through several counties near Albany, a young man named Joseph Whaley had a somewhat violent encounter with an animal he said reminded him of a gorilla. Whaley was on the Bronwood-Smithville Highway cutting grass and brush. He was working with a scythe when he heard a strange noise. Going into the woods to investigate what had caused the commotion, Whaley encountered a six-foot-tall animal covered with shaggy gray hair. Whaley said that the animal had tusk-like teeth and was heard to make noises that sounded like a grunting pig. Obviously frightened by the animal, Whaley swung his scythe at it, making contact with its chest and arm. This did not deter the animal, for it kept coming toward Whaley, who then fled to his jeep so that he could call for help on his radio. Failing to get through to anyone who could help him, Whaley then found himself having to defend himself against the creature; the beast was soon upon him, and in the scuffle, the animal scratched him and ripped his shirt. Whaley decided to get out of the jeep and use it as a buffer between him and the animal, and shortly after doing so, he ran into the woods, where he lost the animal and was able to return to his jeep and drive away.[68]

Perhaps one of the most interesting Bigfoot encounters in Georgia came from Fulton County, the most populous county in the state and possibly the least likely of all places where a Bigfoot would be seen. In 1961, a group of children were playing in the grass behind their house. The area was near Campbellton Road, and the witness described the environment as farmland with pine forests. Considering that the year of the sightings was 1961, it is not inconceivable that the area would be heavily forested, as the growth of modern Atlanta had not reached all parts of Fulton County at that time. It appears that as the children were playing, they were frightened by what they thought was a gorilla that was underneath the house in what the witness called an unfinished basement. The children threw rocks at the animal, and it simply smiled at them. Although they initially thought it was a gorilla, they were quite stunned as they examined it closer and saw that it had a human-like face. They described the creature as being docile, and even smiling. It appears that this was not the only encounter the family or its neighbors had with the animal; in fact, the witness indicated that his family believed there were a number of these animals living in the woods nearby. The witness reported that there were footprints and indentions in the ground discovered near their home quite frequently, and that the creature apparently took on the role of a peeping Tom, as the witness said that the family reported seeing red eyes peering in the windows of the house from time to time. Other activity included one of these creatures stealing chicken eggs from the family chicken coop, and on occasion, the animals could be seen eating apples from a nearby orchard.[69]

A few years later, in 1963, on the opposite end of the state on Jekyll Island located in Glynn County, a seventeen-year-old boy and his brother were driving around the island during the July 4th holiday. Having just gotten a driver's license, the boy decided to go for a drive and spend some time looking around the island instead of driving to the north end to see the local fireworks display. After turning off the main road onto a dirt path, he saw the creature as it stepped out of the woods nearby. The animal, described as being around 5½ feet tall and covered with grayish hair, stood in the beams of the headlights, allowing the youngster to get a good look. After a moment, it walked off into the woods on the other side of the road. As the witness described his encounter to an investigator, he mentioned that the creature had arms that were much longer than humans and that it looked as if it weighed much the same as a human of that height would. He also mentioned that the animal's eyes glowed with a yellow-green color when the headlights of the car hit them. The witness also mentioned that he felt that this particular animal was young.[70]

In 1966, near the town of Whigham located in Grady County near the Florida border, a group of campers did not see the animal itself, but heard a powerful scream that they felt could only have come from something like a Bigfoot. The group included five people who were camping near Wolf Creek. While sitting by the campfire waiting to check fishing nets they had placed in the creek, the group heard splashing in the water down-creek near the nets. Two of the five went to investigate and check their nets for fish. Near the creek, they heard what sounded like large tree limbs breaking, followed by a scream, which they described as being so loud that it jarred the ground. The two decided to return to the camp area quickly, as the scream was a kind they had never heard before.[71]

Near Stellaville, a small town near Augusta, a teenager and her twelve-year-old cousin were walking in a creek near Ways Baptist Church in September 1973. The two heard shuffling and grunting when the twelve-year-old spotted what was thought at first to be a big hairy man in the woods nearby. The witness reported that the two must have scared the animal, which they said looked like a "big man in an overcoat," because as they looked back while running they saw the animal hurrying away from the creek as well. The animal looked like it had hair hanging all around his body. The two told their story to one of the youngster's fathers and an uncle, who proceeded to walk back to the area and look around. The men told the children that they more than likely had disturbed an old drunk sleeping it off in the woods. However, one of the witness's mothers was not so sure. She attributed the sighting to an area legend called the "Bullis Man" or "wild man" that she used to hear about as a teenager in the 1930s. The witnesses commented that neither of them knew exactly what they had seen, but that it was very large and ran away from them deeper into the swampy part of the woods.[72]

In 1974, a woman was riding a horse in Douglas County when she encountered a Bigfoot in the woods about twenty miles from the ranch where she was paid to ride horses. It was getting dark during a full moon when the woman was riding the horse on a dirt road. After crossing a wooden bridge, the rider heard a loud scream and noticed a pair of green eyes staring at her from the woods nearby. The animal to which those bright green eyes belonged jumped out of the woods and lunged at her and the horse she was riding. The animal grabbed the saddle and the back of the horse, forcing the rider to jump on the neck of the horse and lose control of the reins. The horse ran quickly and apparently left the animal behind in the dust. The rider came very close to the creature, describing it as "face to face." Among the things that shocked her was that the animal had hands instead of paws, and that when it grabbed the saddle, it left a deep gash. She described the animal as tall, covered with hair, and having teeth, although some were missing. The animal left the horse and saddle in such disarray that when the woman returned to the ranch the next day to check on the horse, the rancher told her that he no longer needed her services.[73] Perhaps this is the only case in Georgia of a Bigfoot costing a person her job.

In 1976, in Effingham County near Savannah, a man was driving in the predawn hours on his motorcycle on an hour-long commute to a construction site where he worked. Shortly after leaving that morning, the man returned home visibly shaken by something that he had seen on the road during his ride. After calming down enough to recount his story, he talked of seeing a tall, hairy creature crossing the road out of a swampy area nearby. Once on the road, the animal stopped after it noticed the cyclist, who had also stopped his bike in case the animal ran back across the road and caused a collision. The animal stood around seven feet tall, and as it stood there in the road, it appeared to lower its head so it could see the rider on the bike beneath the headlight of the cycle. The man was so shaken by the incident that he could hardly speak once he returned home that morning. It was also quite difficult to discuss the incident thereafter, as it would give him goose bumps and a lump in his throat. The individual's grandfather also discussed seeing what he called "swamp monkeys" that he thought roamed the area around the Savannah, Ogeechee, and Altamaha River areas.[74]

That same year, a man who was hunting and checking his catfish lines on the Alapaha River in Berrien County encountered an animal he was neither hunting nor trying to catch on a catfish line. While he was checking the line, he heard heavy, raspy breathing nearby. Along with the curious breathing, the man also smelled a foul odor in the air. At that point, he decided to leave the area, and as he backed away toward his truck, he saw the animal from a distance of about ten feet. Described as about six feet tall, wet, and having green slime on one of its legs, the animal stopped when it saw the man, who decided that it was time to quickly leave the area. He described the animal as looking like a man covered with fur. Its forehead was bare, and it had a wide nose. The witness also reported that his uncle, who had lived in the area since the 1930s, had seen these animals in groups, and that they would steal melons and sweet corn from his farm.[75]

Perhaps the most intriguing group of sightings happened around 1979 in the southwestern portion of the Atlanta metro area near the city of Newnan. Located in Coweta County, Newnan is now a fast-growing suburb of Atlanta, but back in the 1970s, the area still had a good bit of undeveloped farmland, even some very near the city of Newnan itself. Belt Road and Belk Road, the area where the sightings happened for what has become known as the "Belt and Belk Road Booger," are on the west side of the city, and this area was not a very well developed part of Coweta County at the time. The stories of the "Belt and Belk Road Booger" were covered by Winston Skinner, a young intern for the *Times-Herald*, the local newspaper in Newnan. Skinner is now one of the news editors for the paper, and vividly remembers covering the saga. According to Skinner, in the summer of 1979 while he was interning for the paper in preparation for a career in journalism, he got a call from some people on Belt Road telling of a creature they had seen near their barn and in other places on their property. Skinner and a photographer visited the location and took photographs of the area.[76] The story that was eventually written by Skinner and released by the paper reported that the sightings of the monster occurred near the intersection of Belt Road and West Washington Street, and that the creature spotted stood about five feet tall, was dark, had a large chest and eyes that glittered like diamonds when a light was shined on them. The encounter frightened the witnesses so much that they called the Newnan police department. Police Chief Jerry Helton responded and came to the area to conduct an investigation. He checked tracks that were supposedly made by the monster on a creek bank near the witness's residence. However, according to Helton, the tracks were unrecognizable and could have been made by a dog. Helton took pictures of the tracks and they were included in the story released by the paper. The eyewitness reported to Skinner that after Helton left the scene, the creature returned. The article also reported that the witness's son had seen the creature during the daylight hours and that it appeared to have gorilla-like features and eyes that shone like silver.[77]

Shortly after the paper ran the story, the newspaper office got a flood of calls. One such call came from a lady who lived in a nearby mobile home park. She claimed that the Belt Road Booger ate plants on her front porch. This time, the newspaper editor accompanied Skinner to the site to interview the witness. The lady described how the monster walked right up to her home, grabbed several of her potted plants, and devoured them as she watched. Skinner commented that the ordeal frightened the woman so much that she actually wet her pants while the creature was having his feast, a comment she made to the editor, with whom she apparently felt more comfortable sharing that part of the story since the editor was also a woman.[78]

Another article ran the following week in the *Times Herald*, this one giving many more details about the sightings reported the previous week. According to one eyewitness, the creature stood around five feet tall and resembled a beaver, with bushy hair and a tail. Apparently, this animal had a fascination with flowers, for it was in her yard trying to dig up her caladiums. Another witness mentioned that the animal was nothing new and had been seen in the Belt Road/Smokey Road area for the last nine years. Others commented that the animal could be heard bellowing in the area at night, and that two mangled dogs and a chicken with a bite in its back were credited to the Belt Road Booger. Some residents told Skinner that their dogs cowered in fear on their porches when the animal was near, and two brothers reported seeing the creature as they were driving in the Wallace Gray-Ishman Ballard Road area one night. They reported that the animal appeared to be the size of a cow and stood on its hind legs. As they approached the booger, it went down on all fours and ran off.

The incidents were causing such a stir that Coweta County Sheriff Aaron Massey commented that the Sheriff's Department planned to set animal traps in the area of the sightings so that the creature could possibly be trapped. An area game warden was reported to have set body traps on behalf of the Georgia Department of Natural Resources for that same purpose.[79] Soon afterwards, sightings of the creature got fewer and fewer, but an article released later that month indicated that an Atlanta man, after reading about the creature in the paper, decided to spend part of his vacation from work tracking the creature. He reported that on one morning, a pack of dogs chased something through the woods in the area, but he never saw what they were chasing or any signs of the Belt Road Booger.[80]

The animal was named by Eddie Ball of the Coweta County Emergency Management Agency. Ball pulled the name from the area where the sightings originated, although some came from Belk Road, which is actually connected to Belt Road and is the name of the southern section of the thoroughfare. Ball commented in a newspaper report that during the years the alleged creature was reported, "lawmen and emergency personnel were flooded with reports of [the] large, hairy, two-legged critter roaming the Belt Road area on Newnan's west side, scaring folks half to death."[81]

The creature became quite popular in Coweta County at the time. In fact, Skinner remembers that the local radio station began running reports that a local resident had captured the creature on film and had brought a picture of it to the station. He said that others in the area commented that local Georgia Department of Natural Resources officers were contacted by their superior officer at the state level and admonished for not investigating the creature and following up on all the sightings. Skinner said he could never confirm whether or not that was true, but does remember quite a few people talking about it in the Newnan area at the time.

Talk of the creature went on for several months, and Skinner remembers people telling him that the whole thing was a hoax.[82] Eddie Ball believes that it was not a hoax, but rather it was a case of mistaken identity. He even told Alex McRae of the *Times-Herald* in an April 2005 report that "the original booger was a man, now deceased, who was very large and a bit strange and shy about being seen walking down the local roads. When cars approached he would duck into a ditch, then reappear and continue his trek to nowhere. He wore a water faucet handle around his neck... and was totally harmless, if a bit eccentric."[83] However, this was just Ball's take on the happenings and many others did not share his opinion, although some treated it as a huge local joke. Skinner even commented that the creature became so popular around Newnan that he remembered seeing a picture of a man who had dressed up as the Belt Road Booger for Halloween the year of the sightings.

Skinner mentioned that he never really found any evidence of the creature himself, but some people claimed to have found prints, although they never brought in a photo or cast of such to the paper office. However, Skinner still thinks there might have been something unusual out there scaring people, not a man in a monkey suit. He mentioned that there were several "normal" people who told him that they had seen something like what was being described as the Belt Road Booger, but that they were reluctant to talk about it for fear of ridicule and ostracism. The articles he wrote did have a lighthearted tone, he said, but many people who called him and talked with him about the sightings and what they had encountered were quite serious and did not see the whole thing as a big joke.[84] Whatever people were seeing and whether or not the Belt Road/Belk Road Booger was actually a Bigfoot, the good news was that no one ever reported being harmed by what they saw, and the Booger was never identified.[85] The reports did attract Bigfoot researchers to the area shortly afterwards, but soon after the reports ran in the summer of 1979, the buzz over the creature subsided and things got back to normal.[86]

In 1982, in Macon County near the town of Oglethorpe, a girl and her family had a scary nighttime encounter with an alleged Bigfoot. The girl, seven years old at the time, shared a bedroom with her brother and her sister, who was a baby and still slept in a crib. The baby's crib was next to the window between the two beds used by the girl and her brother. One night, the seven-year-old was awakened by the sound of grunts outside the bedroom window. The baby was standing up in her crib, and had obviously been awakened by the grunts as well. It appeared that the baby was responding to the animal and its grunts, as the baby seemed to be grunting back to it. The young girl never saw the animal on that occasion, but seemed to think that it was quite large. However, nine years later, the entire family would get an opportunity to see their visitor clearly as it came face to face with the mother as she went outside to tend to the family dogs. The animal was about six feet tall, and when the mother saw the animal, the two of them stood paralyzed in fear of one another. After a few seconds, the mother screamed and ran indoors for her husband, and the animal ran off after hearing the mother scream. Apparently it returned, for when the woman entered the house and recounted the event to her husband, he grabbed his gun and then watched through the bathroom window as the animal got close to the house. A few moments later, he shot at the creature through the bathroom wall, hitting it and causing it to scurry off into the woods. Later, another one of the creatures returned to the yard throwing objects. The family reported that it appeared angry, perhaps because the father had shot the other Bigfoot moments earlier. The family also reported that they had other encounters with the creatures. The grandmother, who was prone to drinking, incautiously approached one of the animals in the yard. On another occasion, one of the creatures got stuck underneath the family's house. The animals were described as having chocolate brown hair with long arms extending almost to their knees.[87]

In 1983, in Twiggs County, not far from the city of Macon, a hunter encountered what seemed to be a Bigfoot near the small community of Dry Branch. He appears to have stumbled upon the creature, reporting that it stood up beside him not more than five feet away and screamed. The sound was ear piercing, according to the witness. The hunter, who was 6'3", reported that the animal stood much taller than he did. After a few moments, the animal walked off, crashing through the bushes. While walking away, the animal roared again, repeating this every fifty yards. Describing the animal as standing close enough to touch him, the hunter commented that he had held a rifle in his hands the entire time but was afraid to fire on it due to its close proximity. Because he had come so close, the hunter assumed that he had disturbed the creature as it slept. Although he was close to the animal, the hunter could not describe it in detail, commenting only that it was massive in size.[88]

A year later, a thirteen-year-old girl had a frightening encounter with an apelike animal in the woods of Clayton County near the town of Riverdale, a southern suburb of Atlanta. The girl was walking home from a friend's house one evening before dark. The area was heavily wooded and was near a lake where a local farmer had two pastures for cattle-grazing. Nearby was a trailer park where the girl's friend lived and from whence she was returning the evening of the encounter. Along the path she was traveling, she came upon her father, who was upset that she was in the woods at such a late hour. The witness, who at the time of making the report was over thirty, remarked that her father had been verbally forceful when he told her and her mother not to be in those woods near or after dark. While this seemed strange to the girl, she quickly realized the importance of that advice once she encountered the animal.

When she left her father on the trail, she heard movement in the brush beside her. After turning and seeing the creature, she began to run quickly toward home, the creature following her and running through the foliage parallel to her path. Once she reached a clearing, she noticed that the animal stopped running alongside her and crouched down near the ground watching her run away. It seemed as if it did not want to leave the clearing to pursue her. What she saw was completely hairy, dark, humanlike, and grunting loudly. She also saw that it had large arms that were as big as a person's thighs. The animal stood around seven to eight feet tall and had a massive chest. The woman also mentioned that she and her family had walked the trails in those woods quite often, and on several occasions they came upon a cow from the local cattle ranchers' farms. Something had killed the cattle and ripped out their stomachs. After the encounter with the animal as it chased her along the path that evening, the witness was afraid to venture into those woods very often, and she continued to heed her father's warning of not being in them at all near dark.[89]

In August 1986 on the Alabama/Georgia border, a man was looking for ginseng when he saw a large creature that he said had a pointed head. The animal was described as having long arms, so long that they hung to its knees. The witness felt that the creature was hurt, because its left arm appeared to be useless. He also said that its hands had "long curved fingernails." Although its right arm looked normal, its left leg seemed injured. The witness further described the creature he saw as covered with thick, long hair that fell in locks. The animal's face had thick lips and a flat nose. The witness observed the animal from about twenty to twenty-five feet away but felt no apparent danger, as the animal simply grunted and walked away from the area.[90]

In 1988, a young man, his father, and a friend were traveling home from his grandmother's house, when two animals not native to northeast Georgia appeared in front of their truck on a rural road in Franklin County. However, it was the second animal that caused the greatest stir. The road on which they were traveling at around 2:00 AM was bordered on both sides by pastures that in turn were surrounded by forests. It was reported that in those woods, turkey and deer could easily be found.

Suddenly, the father slammed on the brakes in the middle of the road
after spotting a wolf in the middle of the highway. The boy's father was
startled because there are no wolves in northeast Georgia, but what was
following the wolf frightened them even more. It was an eight-foot-tall,
manlike creature with grayish-brown shaggy hair. After looking at the
people in the truck, the creature gracefully jumped over a four-foot-high
barbed-wire fence and ran into the pasture. Shortly after reaching the
pasture, the animals stopped, turned to look at the truck, and then ran off
out of sight. While in the truck, the boy and his friend were crying and
screaming for the father to drive away, but he was too mesmerized by
what he saw to leave the area so quickly. The boy reported that there was
a foul odor in the air as the animal crossed the road. In addition, he said
that the creature's eyes glowed like amber, and that it moved with the
grace and agility of an Olympic runner.[91]

Sightings of creatures most commonly attributed to Bigfoot have
quite a history in Georgia after the advent of Europeans. Since
newspapers were not common in the state, and most people in the 1800s
and early 1900s were reluctant to come forward with what they had seen
for fear of ridicule and ostracism, there were few recorded sightings in
Georgia during that era. In addition, many people might have seen these
animals and mistaken them for bears or other familiar creatures of the
forest. However, as society, technology, attitudes, and science began to
advance, things changed. With the coming of the 1990s and the advent of
the Internet and easily accessible worldwide communications, reports of
Bigfoot/Sasquatch sightings all over the world increased, Georgia
included. In the mid 1990s, one Bigfoot encounter in Georgia would lead
to the discovery of a footprint that would count as proof that the
creatures did exist beyond the Rocky Mountains, and specifically in the

southeastern United States. In addition, it would launch Bigfoot research careers for several individuals and lead to the development of the largest website devoted entirely to the tracking of Bigfoot in the state of Georgia.

4
The Elkins Creek Cast: Crown Jewel of Georgia Sasquatchery

In terms of research done on strange and mysterious phenomena, every mystery has its encounter or sighting that is considered the crown jewel of its particular field. For example, the crash at Roswell, New Mexico, is considered the big event in UFO research. Along those same lines, Nessie is the pinnacle of the search for underwater sea creatures, and the Patterson/Gimlin footage is the critical piece of evidence for the existence of Bigfoot. Georgia sasquatchery has its own crown jewel, and, fortunately, this piece of evidence is also important to Bigfoot research in general. That jewel was a plaster cast made of a track left by what is thought to have been an elderly male Bigfoot in Pike County, not far from Griffin. The track is now known as the Elkins Creek cast.

The story of the Elkins Creek cast is best told by Steve Hyde of Georgia Bigfoot. According to Hyde, he first learned of the cast and the incident from which it came when he and a few friends, one of whom was former Pike County deputy sheriff James Akin, gathered routinely at a local pawn shop in the town of Griffin, Georgia, a town in Spaulding County not far from Pike County and about forty-five minutes south of downtown Atlanta. Hyde related to Akin that he had always been interested in strange and mysterious phenomenon and happened to be a Bigfoot enthusiast. At that time, Akin began discussing a cast made from a track found in Pike County when he had responded to a call from an elderly man who lived there near Elkins Creek. Akin related that he was not sure what animal made the track, but that it was quite unusual and not from any animal with which he was familiar. Hyde finally convinced Akin to bring the cast into town so he could see what it was all about. According to Hyde, his curiosity was more than piqued when Akin told him the details of how the cast was made.[92]

According to Akin, the Pike County Sheriff's Department had over time received quite a few calls from this elderly gentleman from the Elkins Creek area. The elderly man was even considered a nuisance by members of the sheriff's department because he often called the office reporting that someone or something was hitting the side of his mobile home. The incidents always seemed to happen after midnight and frequently made the dogs on the property very uneasy and chaotic.[93] The intruder also stole dog food and disturbed the gentlemen's property. When the complaint was called in on the day the cast was made, the gentleman even mentioned that the door to his corncrib had been torn off during the night. When Akin arrived, he discovered that there was indeed a mess at the scene of the incident.[94]

The old man described the nature of the incidents to Deputy Akin, but emphasized that the overnight attack had not been the only one and that these events had been occurring over the course of the last few years. He described the attacker as using incredible force as he, she, or it pounded a fist on the side of the mobile home. In addition, Deputy Akin learned that the person or animal causing the problem would routinely harass the old man's dogs, and had on occasion even killed a few of them. The old man described incidents where the intruder would howl and "huff" outside the trailer, and would oftentimes shadow him by following along as he walked inside the length of his trailer. He even reported that the assailant would seem to whisper to him and was likely getting really close to the exterior wall of the trailer on the outside to do so. The whole scene was a bit overwhelming to Akin when he visited. He described what he saw to Sam Rich at Georgia Bigfoot:

> It was my assumption that someone local was harassing him. Honestly, he had a grating personality. He was gruff and tended to speak his mind. These traits do not normally enhance one's social life. However, he did seem truthful. It was at this point I began to explore the possibility that the situation was not a normally explainable events [sic]. I saw the result of these nightly visits. I witnessed the telltale signs of his malevolent, nightly intruder. I saw the fifty-pound dog food sacks emptied in one sitting. I smelled the rotting, pigpen aroma of this intruder as it hung in the cool night air. I examined the multiple dents in his mobile home. I saw a tractor tire thrown into a tree (no mean feat), and, of course, I saw his remorse over the dogs — which were often ripped to pieces.[95]

After talking to the man, Akins felt that it could have been a group of moonshiners who were reported to be active along the Elkins Creek area that was very near the gentleman's home. Akins felt that more than likely this was a case of those moonshiners trying to scare off the old man so that he would not see and be able to report on their illegal activities. The old man then asked Deputy Akins if he wanted to see and know what he felt was really causing all the problems. The gentlemen agreed to show Akin, as long as he did not make fun of him or react negatively to what he was about to reveal. At such time, the man walked Deputy Akins behind his trailer into the wooded area leading to the creek. There, the man showed Akins five prints. Four were in the creek itself and covered with water, while the other one was alongside the creek above water. The cast was made from the one above water.[96] Akin mentioned that the prints were on a small island in the middle of the creek and that the island was shaped like an Australian boomerang. The prints were rather large, and when he first caught sight of them, he felt afraid and even surveyed the area around the creek to make sure that the intruder who made them was no longer in the vicinity.

Still feeling that the entire thing was a hoax, Akin decided to make plaster casts of the only print that he could reach, the one that was on the side of the creek bank. Akin felt that the prints were recent, perhaps only a few hours old. The print was made in ground that was a combination of river sand and clay. The area also had quite a bit of decaying plant matter and the soil was moist, which Akin mentioned made it much easier to catch the dermal ridges in the cast, which are the line patterns ingrained in the skin of primates and humans on the soles of their feet and the palms of their hands. As he began to reassess the events, Akin was not so sure anymore that this was a hoax.[97]

According to Akin, the intrusions ceased shortly after the cast was made. It should be noted that the older man moved from the area, which Akins felt removed the animal's food source, causing it to move to another area possibly closer to the nearby Flint River to look for more food.[98] Some in the area who remembered the series of events mentioned that the elderly man's wife had grown tired of the incidents. She was quite frightened by what was happening to her and her husband's home as it was attacked in the middle of the night. Perhaps this was a contributing factor to the couple's decision to move. The events had been taking place previous to the cast being taken sometime around 1994. The elderly gentleman who reported these incidents at Elkins Creek is now deceased.[99]

After learning of these events, Hyde convinced Akin to allow him to send the cast to Dr. Grover Krantz at Washington State University.[100] Dr. Krantz was a professor of anthropology at the university, and was well known for his work on human evolution. He is credited by longtime Bigfoot researcher and cryptozoologist Loren Coleman as being the first real academic to put his career and reputation on the line for Bigfoot research. Coleman points to Dr. Krantz's high academic credentials and the respectability of his work on human evolution to explain why many in the academic world would not brush aside his research and theories on the existence of Bigfoot/Sasquatch. Krantz had been part of the Bigfoot research field since he was asked to examine the casts of a print found in Colville, Washington, in 1968. A skeptic at first, he found evidence in the print that whatever had made it had a broken bone, something that could not have been fabricated by a hoaxer. Later, he examined prints from the Walla Walla area, and in these prints, dermal ridges were found. Krantz became a believer and devoted a good part of his career to this research, so much so that he was unable to devote as much time to securing grants, which could have hurt his chances at getting tenured at Washington State University. He died in 2002 of pancreatic cancer.[101]

In addition to sending the print to Dr. Krantz, Steve Hyde also sent it to Dr. Jeffrey Meldrum of Idaho State University.[102] Like Krantz, Meldrum had spent much time researching Bigfoot. Dr. Meldrum is a professor of anatomy and anthropology at ISU, and his academic career is built on his study of primate movement and how humans came to walk upright on two legs. He is the author of a number of books about primates, as well as what has become a must-read for Bigfoot enthusiasts, *Sasquatch: Legend Meets Science*. In addition, he is also the affiliate curator at the Idaho Museum of Natural History.[103]

Dr. Meldrum's interest in Bigfoot did not come as an abrupt transition from his academic work and studies. He grew up in Spokane, Washington, where he saw Roger Patterson's film as a young boy. He was fascinated by all things prehistoric, but his youthful interest in Bigfoot became dormant as he pursued his graduate school training in zoology at Brigham Young University and physical anthropology at the State University of New York at Stony Brook. What brought this interest back was his discovery of what he thinks are Bigfoot prints at Walla Walla, Washington. Those tracks were fresh when he first encountered them, and he was amazed at the number of them that were there at one time. There were around thirty to forty along the side of a muddy road. After this event, he became very persistent in his interest. According to Dr. Meldrum, "Seeing these tracks shifted Bigfoot in my mind from the occult to biology, and gave me the same kind of sensation I had when I first held a prehistoric fossil in my hand." He felt that his background and prior research gave him an opportunity to comment on the Bigfoot phenomenon and do credible research.[104]

Dr. Krantz and Dr. Meldrum had seen casts from east of the Rocky Mountains before, but they all had pretty much been human prints or identifiable animal prints. However, the Elkins Creek cast withstood the rigorous academic tests that the two put it through. Both Krantz and Meldrum tested the cast. Dr. Meldrum commented that "Steve's print was remarkably consistent with prints taken of the creature in the Pacific Northwest. In the Elkins Creek cast, there were dermal ridge patterns in parts of the cast."[105]

Dr. Meldrum says that even though he is quite sure that the cast from Elkins Creek is authentic and from an animal that could very well be a Bigfoot, there is always room for misinterpretation, but he is pretty sure that the print is not a hoax. He also mentioned that since a deputy sheriff made the cast of the print, this adds extra weight to the argument for its authenticity. However, Meldrum says he cannot know for sure all the facts concerning the track, because he was not the one to find it. He commented that the print from Elkins Creek was in good shape and had been altered very little from the original print when he got it, but there were some features of the cast that looked as though some cleaning up had been done: removing rocks or sticks that had been in the print, or perhaps shaping parts of the cast back into place. Nonetheless, according to Dr. Meldrum, this does not take away from the purity of the cast and its authenticity. This type of clean-up activity invariably leaves human marks on a cast, but the overall anatomy, shape, and proportions make it very likely that the cast is authentic.[106]

Dr. Krantz's assessment of the cast was quite similar to that of Dr. Meldrum. He believed that the print was indeed from an animal. In his estimation, the animal that made the print was an old adult male. He reached this conclusion because, according to his examination, the bottom of the foot had lost a considerable amount of fat. Humans and primates store fat on the bottom of their feet to pad their walk and to absorb the impact the foot makes when it hits the ground. Dr. Krantz felt that the Bigfoot/Sasquatch creature was no different in this aspect. He even went so far as to hypothesize that the animal that made the Elkins Creek tracks was possibly starving due to tooth loss, which is common among older specimens and would help to explain the loss of fat on the bottom of the foot. This could also explain why the animal was so aggressive in taking food from the residence of the older man in Pike County where the print was made. Although he felt comfortable with his assessment, Dr. Krantz, like Meldrum, remained cautious, because he too had not been part of the harvesting of the print and did not know the context from which it came.[107]

A while after examining the cast, Dr. Meldrum sent it to Jimmy Chilcutt, who at the time was employed by the Conroe Police Department in Conroe, Texas.[108] Chilcutt, who has garnered the respect and high recommendations of the FBI for his work on fingerprint analysis, is an expert in nonhuman primate prints. Before becoming a Bigfoot researcher himself, he was a hard-nosed skeptic who tried to use his expertise to debunk, not prove, Bigfoot's existence. During the course of his research, he reached the conclusion that while not all the prints brought forth are legitimate, many are and are indeed the prints of an elusive animal yet to be recognized by modern science. He met Dr. Meldrum when he flew to Idaho State University in Pocatello, Idaho, to begin studying prints in Meldrum's collection. He had contacted Dr. Meldrum earlier after hearing the professor discuss his research on a television show. Chilcutt's interest was piqued when he heard Meldrum refer to dermal ridges on these prints, a term that is unmistakably identified with fingerprints. When he contacted Meldrum, he asked to come and use his expertise to try and eliminate prints that were fakes. The print that Chilcutt first examined was the one Meldrum was using on the television show Chilcutt had seen and about which he had contacted the professor. That print was a fake, because the alleged toe-prints were easily identified as human. However, on more than a few of the prints Dr. Meldrum had in his possession, Chilcutt found that the dermal ridges ran lengthwise up and down the foot. Human dermal ridges run side to side, and Chilcutt knew that these prints were not human. Not long afterwards, Chilcutt became a bona fide believer and began devoting some of his time to Bigfoot research.[109]

Chilcutt's expertise in this field was unquestionable to Hyde and others. After examining the cast, he determined that the Elkins Creek print was indeed that of a nonhuman primate. Chilcutt divided the Elkins Creek print into four areas: after examining each area, he concluded that two of them showed clear indications that the animal making the print was nonhuman and was not an identified primate. He measured the print to be 17.5 inches long and 8.5 inches wide. His findings were submitted via report to Dr. Meldrum.[110]

After getting a copy of the results of Jimmy Chilcutt's examination, Steve Hyde began posting comments on various Bigfoot Internet forums on the web; he even sent George Karras, a Bigfoot researcher in Oregon, a copy of the Chilcutt report. This is when the cast and incident began to get nationwide attention. After examining the cast, both Dr. Meldrum and Jimmy Chilcutt included the Elkins Creek cast and their findings concerning it in the presentations on Bigfoot/Sasquatch that they give at schools and conventions around the nation. The Elkins Creek cast excited both Meldrum and Chilcutt because it correlated in terms of dermal ridges and prints with casts found in the Pacific Northwest. They both agreed that the cast would help prove that the creature was real and was present in other states.[111]

Before the Elkins Creek phenomena, there had been very little credence given to the possibility of Bigfoot east of the Rockies. Once the Elkins Creek cast came up, it proved to Krantz, Chilcutt, and Meldrum that there was activity elsewhere. Now, most all of the people involved in Bigfoot research acknowledge that Bigfoot is probably a national phenomenon, not just a Pacific Northwest one. In addition, according to Hyde, the Elkins Creek cast is not only valuable in that it proves that these creatures could exist in the southeastern United States and other places east of the Rocky Mountains, it also proves something else in the broader context of Bigfoot research. Hyde related that there are only about seven pieces of evidence in existence that the North American Bigfoot exists as a real creature. The Patterson/Gimlin film footage is one, and the other six are casts. One of the six casts is from the Elkins Creek print.[112] Meldrum agreed with this assessment.[113]

While there have been many sightings, encounters, and prints taken in Georgia of what researchers call Bigfoot or Sasquatch, the Elkins Creek cast stands out among them. Not only did it draw the attention of three of the Bigfoot world's most notable figures, it also opened the door to more research in the state. Shortly after the cast was made available to Steve Hyde, it made such an impression on him that he and a few other friends became heavily involved in Georgia Bigfoot, conducting field research and collecting evidence in an attempt to prove this animal's existence. These men and a host of others from Northeast Georgia to the coast near Savannah and the Barrier Islands, spend time, resources, and energy in pursuit of these Georgia giants. The Elkins Creek cast is the crown jewel in the treasure chest of evidence collected in Georgia thus far.

5

Organizations and Field Researchers

With the advent of the Internet, information has become readily available to one and all. Students everywhere have become more and more dependent on the Internet for their school research, as well as for leisurely reading, gaming, and interpersonal communication. In addition, the Internet has provided an impetus for those who are interested in various things to engage in research and pursue their interests. Although it is advisable to be cautious as to what can be used on the Internet as reliable information, no one can argue the point that the web has changed the way the world gets its information and explores new territory.

As well as providing an opportunity for research, the Internet has also offered countless people the opportunity to come forward with sightings and encounters that they have had with the creature many call Bigfoot. There is a certain cloak of anonymity to the Internet, and most organizations that collect information on sightings and encounters provide that anonymity to their subscribers. A simple search of the Internet will produce more than a couple of dozen websites catering to the Bigfoot community, and, of those, almost all of them have databases of sightings collected from people who write in and report their encounters or sightings of tracks and other evidence attributed to the creature.

In terms of Georgia sasquatchery, several of the larger Bigfoot databases include sightings from all fifty states, although many do not list any sightings from Hawaii, even though space is allotted in the event that reports do come in from the Aloha State. In addition to these larger databases, there are also a few sites devoted purely to research in Georgia, sightings in Georgia, and ongoing field research in the state. One of those sites is http://www.georgiabigfoot.com, which as mentioned earlier, is operated by those who were instrumental in bringing forth the Elkins Creek cast. I will elaborate more on this site in this chapter. However, a look at the larger research organizations and their databases, in addition to those devoted entirely to Georgia, will show that there is certainly credible ongoing activity in Georgia relating to the Bigfoot phenomenon.

Of the large organizations that actively engage in field research and keep current databases of sightings, the Bigfoot Field Researchers Organization is perhaps the largest and most active. The group keeps an active website located at http://www.bfro.net. The organization was founded in 1995 by Matt Moneymaker, who currently lives in San Juan Capistrano, California. Born in the 1960s, Moneymaker grew up in

Hollywood Hills, California, the son of a successful bankruptcy attorney. Pursuing a degree in law, he graduated from the University of Akron in Ohio.[114]

Moneymaker has been interested in Bigfoot for a long time. A childhood interest led him to documentaries and books on Bigfoot, and finally to those who were believers themselves. Moneymaker had his first encounter with the alleged creature in 1994 when he was still a law student at the University of Akron. While out with a guide in the woods, he saw a seven-foot creature coming out of the forest. He reported that the creature growled at him, and commented that, "It was almost like an old man, a raspy, deep growl. It was warning me."[115]

The year after his encounter, Moneymaker started the Bigfoot Field Researchers Organization. Currently, the BFRO, as it is commonly called, does about a dozen expeditions around the country every year. The fee for participation in these expeditions is $300 per person and does not include food, transportation, or shelter. The fee pays for the experience that field guides provide, getting participants to areas that have been rich in sightings. On the trips, participants also benefit from the knowledge of researchers who are members of the BFRO.[116] In Georgia, there have been a few expeditions to the north Georgia mountains, an area that has produced numerous sightings and from which various reports have been made to the BFRO.

According to the organization's website, the mission of the BFRO is "multifaceted, but the organization essentially seeks to resolve the mystery surrounding the Bigfoot phenomenon, that is, to derive conclusive documentation of the species' existence."[117] The organization maintains a database of sightings that people have sent in to the BFRO. Once these reports come in, the BFRO responds by investigating them in a manner reminiscent of that employed by those in law enforcement, the legal profession, and investigative journalism. Among the members of the BFRO who investigate reports and sightings are professional trackers and wildlife biologists. Investigators at least follow up these reports by phone, but, in many cases, the investigators visit the witnesses and the sites where evidence has been seen or encounters have taken place. Not all reports are released to the public via the database. Many are not released due to lack of evidence or because there is too much room for error. In other words, some people who report that they have seen a Bigfoot or its tracks have indeed seen another kind of animal, or tracks belonging to an animal known to science.[118]

A few years after Moneymaker launched his organization, the BFRO got an unexpected gift. It came in the form of financial backing from an unlikely donor. His name is Wally Hersom, and he is the former owner of HC Power, a company that manufactured power conversion equipment for cell-phone towers and industrial facilities. He came upon the BFRO website and was very interested in the organization's work. Shortly afterwards, he went on an expedition in Wisconsin, but nothing happened. On a second expedition, Hersom was able to experience what he calls howls of a Bigfoot piercing the night. On that same trip, he also had rocks thrown at him, and he heard three distinct footsteps near his tent in the camp. Since that time, he has accompanied the BFRO on several expeditions and has also purchased his own cameras so that he can hopefully capture footage of the alleged creature. Indeed, he became so enthralled with the work and mission of the BFRO that he has become quite a huge benefactor to the organization. In 2000, he sold his company and netted $110 million. He has used some of that fortune to indulge his fantasy of finding the elusive Bigfoot. Hersom pays the salary of Matt

Moneymaker, and he has given the BFRO ten thermal imaging cameras, video recorders, and night vision devices, all to the tune of about $100,000 in equipment donations.[119]

The BFRO has attracted a number of visitors to its website over the years, and many participants sign up to go on its expeditions. The group has also been affiliated with some of the most well known academics in the field of Bigfoot research, including Dr. Jeffrey Meldrum of Idaho State University who examined the Elkins Creek cast. In his book *Sasquatch: Legend Meets Science*, Dr. Meldrum discusses the BFRO:

> For a time the BFRO took the lead among a new generation of amateur professional investigators. There were a number of organizations of various stripes, but the BFRO boldly touted the distinction of being "the only scientific organization probing the Bigfoot/Sasquatch mystery." A rather grandiose assertion perhaps, but, insofar as efforts were made by its investigators to adhere to the principles and methods of scientific research during the collection, handling, and evaluation of objective evidence, that standard was applied with varying success.[120]

Meldrum does go on to say that the organization, like any other, has its colorful characters, conflicting agendas, and adherents holding strong opinions who are not always open to others, but that there is a noticeable amount of cooperation and professionalism in its membership ranks, among which are individuals "motivated by a conviction that eventually well-documented evidence will bear out their own experiences or convictions and resolve for them a vexing and persistent mystery."[121]

The BFRO has approved investigators in Georgia, and the fact that their database lists almost sixty sightings from at least thirty-eight counties indicates why. The list of counties includes Atkinson, Bartow, Berrien, Brantley, Brooks, Carroll, Cherokee, Clarke, Clayton, Cobb, Coweta, Dade, Douglas, Fannin, Floyd, Fulton, Glynn, Gwinnett, Hall, Haralson, Heard, Lanier, Lee, Liberty, Long, Murray, Paulding, Polk, Rabun, Richmond, Stephens, Stewart, Sumter, Tattnall, Upson, Walker, White, and Whitfield. Among their investigators in Georgia is Leigh Culver, who has been on four BFRO expeditions, two in North Carolina and one in South Carolina, and is also credited as a primary organizer of a 2008 outing in Georgia. Culver has over thirty-five years of outdoor experience and is a professional tracker; he is also a tracking, survival, land navigation, primitive skills, and nature awareness instructor. His primary interest is in military personnel who might have had a Bigfoot/Sasquatch encounter. In addition to Culver, the BFRO also uses several other trackers and investigators from Georgia.[122]

While not as large or well known as the BFRO, the Gulf Coast Bigfoot Research Organization also maintains a database of sightings from across the nation, although their primary research area is the South, mostly regions near the Gulf Coast. As such, they have experienced investigators assigned to each area. Bobby Hamilton of Texas founded the GCBRO, as it is commonly called, in February 1997.[123] Hamilton, a former professional wrestler, had his first encounter with Bigfoot as a child. According to Hamilton, when he was five years old, the creature came to the window of his bedroom and motioned for him to come outside. Hamilton also mentions that his brothers and sisters experienced similar incidents. He speculates that the Bigfoot might have been looking for a quick meal, which was why it was motioning for him, a small child at the time, to come outdoors. Another theory was that it was a female creature that had lost one of its young and wanted a replacement. While these ideas are only conjecture, Hamilton does go on to state that in a year's time, the creature had managed to scare his family so much that they moved from their farm, which was located in Nagocdoches County, Texas. The animal reportedly killed one of the family's pet calves, and an article in the *Houston Press* also reports that, "Monstrous screams in the night and loud banging on the house terrified his mother and aunt, he remembers. The family's perfectly good horse went crazy — Hamilton believes from terror — and could no longer be ridden."[124] The animal scared Hamilton so much that he began sleeping in a sleeping bag with a knife in his hand, a tomahawk under his pillow, and a baseball bat by his side. It became so bad that his mother would have to yell out his name from his bedroom door and wake him before approaching him in his sleep for fear that he would awaken and attack her.[125] It is not difficult to see the impact the sighting at the window and later events on his farm had on Hamilton.

Hamilton started the GCBRO when he realized that a lot of research was being carried on by field researchers and experts in the Pacific Northwest, but that very little attention was being given to the many sightings in other places, specifically the Gulf Coast area. According to the group's website at http://www.gcbro.com, they "joined forces to turn all this around and to bring to light more encounters and happenings from the South. And shed some positive light on a long history of these creatures in the South."[126] Hamilton started the website after he purchased a guidebook on HTML and learned how to build web pages. Hamilton and the GCBRO maintain a listing of sightings from around the country. In addition, they lead expeditions into the woods where sightings have taken place, and even have a page for the submission of sightings and other strange events. The GCBRO web page is also filled with pictures and sketches submitted by visitors to the site and researchers associated with the group.

Currently on the site are reported sightings sent in to the GCBRO from twenty-one of the 159 counties in Georgia, including Dade, Floyd, Grady, Chattahoochee, Forsyth, White, Polk, Franklin, Effingham, Cherokee, Gilmer, Putnam, Troup, Paulding, Lanier, Barrow, Rabun, Bulloch, Fayette, and Morgan counties. As of February 2008, the site included twenty-nine sightings from Georgia, and one of the investigators who follows up on sightings in the state is Bob Wilson.[127]

Although the BFRO and GCBRO do have investigators who cover sightings and follow up on evidence in Georgia, one site in particular is dedicated to searching for the creature exclusively in Georgia. There is no particular name for the group that runs the site. Most people simply refer to them as Georgia Bigfoot, perhaps in reference to the title of their web page, Georgia Bigfoot, located at http://www.georgiabigfoot.com. The site is now maintained by Steve Hyde, who was partially responsible for bringing the Elkins Creek cast to light, and Mike Bankston. The two took over ownership of the site from Sam Rich, who moved out west and was not able to maintain it. Both Bankston and Hyde continue their individual field research, and, according to Bankston, both he and Hyde have an active research site. In addition to maintaining GeorgiaBigfoot.com, the two are also members of the Alliance of Independent Bigfoot Researchers, and Bankston is a moderator at http://www.bigfootforums.com, a site where anyone can register, post, and discuss Bigfoot-related topics.[128]

Hyde, who holds a degree in engineering from Georgia Tech, conducts field research about twice a month. He confines most of his research to the central and south Georgia areas, and his research focuses mainly on pinpointing areas in the state where the animal could survive. He and his research partners concentrate on long-term research in those areas. His most notable discovery besides the Elkins Creek cast was a sighting in Pike County. On this outing in March 1999, Hyde and a few other investigators were exploring the woods of Pike County near Zebulon, Georgia, not too far from the Elkins Creek sighting. While on this excursion, Hyde captured what he calls a "blobsquatch" on film. The picture he took shows a black mass that appears to take the form of a head, arms, and shoulders. While the object is not totally discernable, it does resemble what has been described as a Sasquatch, but since it still has the look of a black blob in the photo, it merits the name "blobsquatch." Hyde posted the picture and an article entitled "Evolution of a Blobsquatch, Another Illustration" on the blog section of Georgia Bigfoot. In the article, Hyde writes:

> My subsequent experience with this photo demonstrated how frustrating blobsquatches could be. I was there at the time, I took the picture, and could see the thing much more clearly than the picture suggests, and the events unfolding at the time strongly suggested to me that … well, it could be. But in the end all I had to show for it was an image of some vague distant "black thing." All analyses done to the image in the photo pointed out some interesting things, but the final objective interpretation was always inconclusive. My initial excitement at capturing an image of what I sure as hell thought at the time was a Bigfoot slowly turned into frustration, then into resignation as I finally realized the photo would never amount to much and was thrown onto the towering heap of maybes. Simply because there wasn't enough

objective detail IN THE PHOTOGRAPH ITSELF to be meaningful. The moral of the story? Photographic evidence has to be of an extraordinarily high quality to warrant any serious attention at all. The photo has to stand on its own merits, regardless of the story that goes with it.[129]

From this article, it is obvious that Hyde's mission is to gather definitive proof that the creature exists in Georgia and in general. According to Hyde, he and his fellow researchers scrutinize the evidence they collect quite meticulously. The scientific method is employed as each piece is examined for authenticity and ability to shed light on the subject. In Hyde's estimation, there is very little to be gained from putting forth evidence that is questionable, and almost as little to be gained from putting forth evidence that proves relatively nothing.[130]

Hyde feels that northern Georgia provides a good habitat for these creatures. In his opinion, development in these areas could possibly be running them out of their habitat and he feels that people could be displacing these creatures, causing them to move about a lot. Growth from the city of Atlanta is more than likely the cause of much movement and migration among these creatures, according to Hyde. If the creature exists, then he feels it is probably the same creature as the ones tramping the woods in the Pacific Northwest. He theorizes that it may have been an animal coming from another part of the world that migrated over time.[131]

Hyde does not feel that the creature poses any real threat to the people of Georgia. He does not remember any reports of a Bigfoot doing any bodily harm to anyone in the state. However, Georgia, like other regions in the nation, does have reports where the animal has broken into a cabin, riffled through the things inside, and upturned property. But there has been no bodily harm or deaths in Georgia directly attributed to these creatures. Hyde does remember one story of a friend of his who would often go out into the wilderness to track the animals by himself. On one occasion, the man was alone and camped by himself in a tent in the woods. While the man was asleep, the creature came fairly close to the tent, stood, and screamed at the top of its lungs. The man woke quickly, figured out what was going on, and decided to move out of the area without delay. He was not chased or harmed as he left. Hyde theorizes that the creature was trying to do just what happened — get the man to leave the area. He says that these creatures can be very territorial. When humans encroach, they sometimes react forcefully, but to date no harm has been reported in Georgia to a person.[132]

Before becoming affiliated with Georgia Bigfoot, Hyde was part of the Georgia Swamp Ape Research Center. Founded in 1995, the GSARC was dedicated to the study of Sasquatch, but it appears from their website that they also studied other animals that might be considered cryptids, such as giant birds and phantom panthers. At some point during its run, the Georgia Swamp Ape Research Center became affiliated with the International Fortean Research Society. This move was made to open up the possibility of increased funding and exposure, as the IFRS dedicated space in its regular newsletter to the Georgia Swamp Ape Research Center. Still appearing on the GSARC web page is an article written by Hyde entitled "Bigfoot and the Apes."[133]

There are other researchers around the state who are not affiliated with any group. Many of them do not wish to be named or mentioned in writing because they have professional reputations to protect and they fear that their jobs and community standing will be jeopardized if the public at large associates them with this field of research. Others in the field do not fear this, but have not joined any research organization. They do accompany more seasoned researchers — usually associated with one of the organizations mentioned in this chapter — instead of organizing themselves into a larger research society or releasing their findings and details of their journeys in writing or on the Web. However, there are thankfully quite a few who do not fear such repercussions and trudge forward in pursuit of knowledge and truth. They come from all walks of life. One Georgian, who regularly sees his name in print, does not shy away from seeing it in print in connection with Bigfoot. As a matter of fact, his research is very well known at his job, among his circle of friends and relatives, and by many newspaper subscribers in the northern Georgia area. We will look at his work in the next chapter.

6

A Journalist Goes on a Search for the Georgia Bigfoot

One thing that most Bigfoot enthusiasts will admit is that stories that appear in the mainstream media about sightings of the alleged creature or tracks left behind generally have a humorous slant to them. Oftentimes, researchers and scientists who spend time looking at possible evidence of the creature are scoffed at and ridiculed by journalists. One need only look at the interview done by *Fox News* with BFRO founder and lead investigator Matthew Moneymaker, where the interviewer, anchors, and set crew can be seen and heard laughing at Moneymaker during and after the interview, after the anchor seemed a bit confrontational with Moneymaker while asking him questions. While it is certainly acceptable for journalists to be skeptical, most would agree that the display seen during this interview was unprofessional and unacceptable — not the way journalists are supposed to approach their subjects in an interview.

This example, as well as others, leads many investigators and scientists in the field to shy away from the media and not rely upon them

Figure 2: Wayne Ford in an area where he frequently travels. An old concrete marker to the right shows this once was a roadbed, now abandoned.

to help further the investigation into the creature's possible existence. This attitude can best be heard in the comments of Robert Morgan of the American Anthropological Research Foundation, an organization that has devoted considerable time and resources to finding Bigfoot, when he commented that when he meets a journalist interested in writing an article about his or the organization's research, he usually does a "backstroke."[134] However, one journalist in Georgia has devoted a portion of his time, both as part of his professional responsibilities and in his spare time, to an objective look at the evidence and to a genuine search for his own evidence that the creatures do actually exist, and indeed live in Georgia. His name is Wayne Ford.

Ford, who holds a bachelor of arts in journalism from the University of South Carolina, is a writer for the *Banner-Herald* in Athens, the home of the University of Georgia. Growing up in Anderson County, South Carolina, bordering on the Peach State and near both Hart and Elbert Counties in Georgia, Ford has always been interested in the topic of Bigfoot. He credits the famous Roger Patterson and his footage of "Patty" for planting the seed of interest in his mind about the possible existence of the creature. As a young man, Ford saw an advertisement in a local paper for Patterson's book *Do Abominable Snowmen of America Really Exist?* and sent away for the volume, which was self-published by Patterson in 1966. Ford still owns that copy of the book.

It was also around that same time that a father and son in Anderson County, South Carolina, reported seeing a "gorilla man" in the woods as they were visiting a sawmill. The two reportedly saw the creature come around the mill, which frightened them both and caused them to leave the area rather quickly. They went into town with their story, returning with a group of men that they hoped would help find the animal. This report circulated a good bit through the Anderson area, and Ford heard about it, as well. He even remembers that as a young boy, he would play in the woods not far from the area where the creature was supposedly sighted.[135]

Now that the Internet has provided a forum for people to report their sightings under the cloak of anonymity, reports like these are quite common. The databases mentioned already in this text have hundreds of such incidents involving "gorilla men," "wild men," "boogers," and "devils." Nevertheless, a couple of decades ago, those who had encountered such creatures were reluctant to discuss them out of fear of being labeled crazy or weird. Those who did risked not only being labeled as such, but also being ostracized, and in some cases thrown out of their churches and social groups.

Even scientists who were interested in the evidence presented by eyewitnesses and hunters passed over the opportunity to get heavily involved, for fear of being ridiculed by other academics and the media, not to mention the damage that could be done to their credibility as scholars. Although more and more academics are coming to the arena or are at least opening their minds to discussing the evidence, many still keep their distance from the field.[136]

For this very reason, Ford became a quiet enthusiast during the 1970s, 1980s, and 1990s. Furthermore, what was being printed about the alleged creature focused mainly on the Pacific Northwest, leading Ford to believe that none of the creatures existed anywhere else. He did not even consider the "gorilla man" story of his youth as related to Bigfoot, thinking that the creatures, if they existed, certainly did not roam the forests and woods of the South. That changed in 2000.[137]

In 1982, Ford came to Athens, Georgia, to accept a position with the *Athens Banner-Herald*. In 2000, he found a website operated by Steve Hyde, who at that time was still involved with the Georgia Swamp Ape Research Center. Ford contacted Hyde and interviewed him in the fall of 2000. In addition to interviewing Hyde, Ford explored the GSARC website, reading articles on the alleged creature and educating himself on the state of Georgia sasquatchery. After spending some time with this, Ford approached the editor of the *Athens Magazine* with the idea of doing a story on Bigfoot sightings in Georgia. He had previously written for the magazine, and had built a positive rapport with the editor. She agreed to allow him to write his story.[138]

The article was published in April 2001, and was entitled "Georgia's Swamp Ape, Fact or Fiction?" In the article, Ford discusses several sightings that had taken place in previous years throughout the state. Included was a sighting involving former University of Georgia student Jason Leathers, who was walking along a path on Skidaway Island on the Georgia coast with a few friends. As they walked, they heard the nearby bushes rustling. Thinking it was possibly a bear, Leathers quickly signaled for his friends to stop and be quiet for fear of startling the animal. It was only when it stood on its hind legs that Leathers and his friends realized they were not looking at a bear. According to the article, "the figure was bipedal and stood close to seven feet tall." Leathers commented that he was frozen for about thirty seconds after the sighting, and, with full agreement from his friends, he decided that it would be best to leave the area quickly. Leathers, who went on to finish a degree in ecology at the University of Georgia and a master's degree in entomology at the University of Kentucky, never discussed the encounter with his friends again. Although he is unsure of what he saw, he did feel certain that it was not a bear.[139]

In the same article, Ford recounts the sighting in 1999 by two young boys in Morgan County. In this encounter, a twelve-year-old Atlanta boy visiting a friend at his parents' home on Lake Oconee encountered an animal standing in the woods. The sighting happened near sundown, and the animal was described as a "towering hair-covered figure." The boys described the look on the animal's face as "mad." Ford writes that, "The creature had a flat face more akin to an ape rather than the snout and face of a bear."[140]

Another sighting mentioned in the article took place a year later in nearby Putnam County in the vicinity of Lake Sinclair, a lake that adjoins Lake Oconee. This incident involved two women, one of whom was Amy Kitchen, a medical transcriptionist hailing from Tallahassee, Florida. One night, Kitchen and one of her friends took a wrong turn, ending up on Blue Fill Road. The women were driving slowly and had their windows down. It was on this road that they saw a creature standing about six feet away from their car as it passed. Ford quotes Kitchen in the article: "The thing was huge. It was really tall and its head looked like it went right down into its shoulders. It didn't have any kind of neck, so to speak. Its arms were larger than normal and kind of thick. It scared me to death." [141]

According to Mike Bankston of Georgia Bigfoot, the creature in Georgia is very similar to the creature tracked in the Pacific Northwest.[142] The description Kitchen gave in her account is quite similar to the description given of the creatures seen in Oregon, Washington State, and Northern California. Ford also writes in the article that sightings in Georgia "have come in from the dense interior of the

Okefenokee Swamp to the rugged remote regions of the north Georgia mountains. There are stories of hunters confronting the creatures, people happening upon huge apelike animals in forested areas, and drivers seeing such animals crossing the road during late hours."[143] The rest of the article recounts the Elkins Creek incident and the research surrounding the Elkins Creek cast carried out by Dr. Jeff Meldrum, Jimmy Chilcutt, and Dr. Grover Krantz.

While writing this article, Ford did not realize that there were as many sightings in the northern Georgia area as there were. According to Ford, "Sometimes you don't find something until you start looking for it."[144] Realizing that the animals might exist right there in the Athens area, he wanted to start looking for them. With the help of Jim Helbert, who now has a blogtalk radio show with Robert W. Morgan, Ford located an area near Athens of about twenty to thirty square miles. Now he has narrowed his search area to only one or two square miles within that perimeter, but at the beginning of his field research, he explored much of the original area.

Ford visits this wooded area quite a bit. Although he does not disclose its location for safety and legal reasons, it is located in northeast Georgia not far from the Athens area. Once he had begun exploring the dense thicket, he started to develop sources that might help him pinpoint specific areas that could lead to evidence — or, even better, an encounter. He contacted landowners, hunters, farmers, and law enforcement officials, all in the hope that they might have seen or heard something strange. He says that it is a weird situation trying to explain what he is doing, but that he is always careful to tell these people that he goes into the woods with a camera and not a gun.[145]

When he first started going into his research area, he did carry a firearm for protection. After becoming more familiar with the research

Figure 3: This is an example of a possible marker found in 2002. Note the limbs on the ground anchoring one end. This is a common feature in these types of markers that might indicate it was purposely done.

done on these creatures, he found that the evidence indicated that these animals probably posed no real threat to humans, and that they more or less wanted to be left alone and stay away from us. He does believe that under the right circumstances the animals can be a threat to humans, but only to defend themselves. He thinks that they are like every other animal who might feel that humans would be a threat to their safety, but he does not think that the creatures are trying to stalk us, only to scavenge and survive. He stated, "They may get close to us if they, for some reason, think humans with which they come in contact are not there to harm them."[146]

When he first started his research in the woods, he did not know anyone else who was interested in searching for Bigfoot in Georgia. To seek out people in the area who might have encountered one of these creatures, he posted signs in area deer-processing plants and small grocery stores. His goal was to get hunters who were in the woods a great deal to come forward with any information that they had. Although no one who had encountered one of the creatures contacted him as a result of the signs and posters, he did meet one other Bigfoot enthusiast in the area. In time, with the publication of an additional article, other enthusiasts and researchers contacted him, and they began to share information with one another.[147]

The article that led to meeting other researchers in the area was published in the *Athens Banner-Herald* on December 13, 2003, and was entitled "Tales of Bigfoot legend include sightings in Georgia — even Clarke County." In this article, Ford discusses the sighting of the alleged creature at the Fort Gordon Army Base near Augusta. The sighting took place in August 1979, and Ford chronicles the events that led to a sighting of some kind of large creature by Jack Hovatter, who happened to be hunting in the woods on the base when he stumbled upon a footprint that he thought at first was a bear track. Mistaking the print for two bear prints, it was his son who corrected him, saying, "No dad, that's one track."

Continuing to think about the track for some time afterward, Hottaver returned to the area a week later to track whatever animal had left the print. Locating a path that led into a thicket near the print he had seen, Hottaver reported, "I got inside and here that thing came. It's not like it was trying to catch me. It was trying to scare me."[148]

According to Ford, "What Hovatter saw was a bipedal apelike creature covered in thick hair. It was about ten feet tall or slightly taller. It came within fifteen feet of him."[149] Hovatter was carrying a shotgun at the time, but felt that the animal was much too big and too close to shoot at. Instead of shooting or immediately running away, Hovatter backed out of the thicket slowly, commenting also that the animal did not appear to be trying to look vicious, although it did have an "ugly" face that made it appear to look stern or that it "meant business." Hovatter did not feel that the animal was human, and disputed the notion by saying that "...although they walk on two legs doesn't mean they are near-human."[150]

In the article, Ford also writes of John Butler, a special education teacher in the metro-Atlanta area, who at the time of the article was working on his doctorate in education. According to Ford, Butler had been interested in the mystery for several years previous to the article, and although at the time he had never seen a Bigfoot, Butler did believe that they existed. Based on his research, Butler told Ford that there is no single Bigfoot, but instead there are many. This, according to Butler, is why there have been reports of the creature in Georgia from the northern reaches of the state all the way to the southern Georgia swamp area.[151]

More interesting, Ford also includes the report of a law enforcement officer near Athens who had an encounter in 1971. The officer, a veteran of over thirty years, reported to Ford that the event happened when he was a young deputy for the Clarke County Sheriff's Department in Athens. He and his partner were summoned to investigate a report of a possible prowler near a trucking business north of the city, which at the time was a rural area that has since been developed and is part of the urban sprawl of the Classic City. When the officers exited their patrol car, the first thing they noticed was a foul odor in the air. They spotted a couple of people on the premises burning something in old drums, but the smell that lingered in the air was not the smoke stemming from their fire. Within moments, someone motioned to the officers that it looked as if something was moving around nearby. Whatever it was seemed to be quite tall, seven to eight feet according to the officer, who also said that it walked like a human. The article went on to say that "...they called the animal a Yeti, a term used mostly for a similar creature alleged to live in the Himalayan mountain range."[152] The officer reported his sighting to others when he returned to the police station, but was ridiculed. This is what has contributed to his decision to remain anonymous.

In 2003, Ford also published a review of a book by longtime Bigfoot researcher Loren Coleman. Coleman's book is entitled *Bigfoot: The True Story of Apes in America*. The article Ford published reviewing the book was "Truisms or Tales? Bigfoot Book Addresses Both." The review appeared in the *Athens Banner-Herald* as well. In the review, Ford writes, "If someone wants one up-to-date book on the subject, this is it.

The book gives us a wonderful overview of the subject..."[153] The review was released the same day as his first article on sightings in Georgia.

On October 3, 2004, yet another review by Ford made its way into the *Athens Banner-Herald*. This one was a review of Christopher Murphy's book *Meet the Sasquatch*. Murphy, a researcher who has spent over a decade in the field, also released *The Bigfoot Film Controversy* a year later in 2005, which was more or less a book that Roger Patterson had published in 1966 and to which Murphy had simply added details about the Patterson/Gimlin footage.[154] In his review, Ford praised *Meet the Sasquatch*, writing, "While not as in-depth as some books on the subject, the book gives the reader an overview of Sasquatch in the culture of Native American Indians and known reports of sightings by the first settlers as they moved to this country... Colorful and compelling, it will give the reader a good idea why this mystery will not go away."[155] Also in the review, Ford mentions that there are sightings of the creature in Georgia and the South, but that Southerners are not given to talking about such things, which is more than likely why sightings in the South rarely make the media.[156] Ford sent a copy of his review to Christopher Murphy, getting back a vote of approval from him for the review as well as pleasant comments about Ford's work.[157]

On February 12, 2006, Ford published another article on Bigfoot in the *Athens Banner-Herald*. This one was entitled "Fact or Fiction on the Hunt." It is an account of a Bigfoot Field Researchers Organization sponsored expedition that was led by the organization's founder and current head, Matthew Moneymaker. The expedition included about twenty people who set out into the woods of the north Georgia mountains in White County, an area that was chosen for the expedition due to the number of sighting reports in northeast Georgia that were sent to the organization. The expedition included people from Mississippi, Illinois, Alabama, South Carolina, Florida, Georgia, and California. During the expedition, Moneymaker and the participants found a pathway where trees had been pruned by an animal or something extremely tall. Another party on the expedition found track signs that were attributed to a bipedal creature with a long stride. While there, the group did not encounter a Sasquatch, but did speak with a resident of nearby Helen who talked to them about her encounter with what she described as a Bigfoot who had crossed a road in a mountain valley in White County. While out in the woods, a couple of the men used a large piece of wood to wood-knock. They also made deep whooping noises to see if they could attract one of the creatures. Two of the men claimed that the creature responded with wood-knocking and a whooping call.[158]

In April of 2006, Ford saw his first Bigfoot print. The print was actually found by someone else when the creature was said to have crossed a dirt road. The print was found in Oglethorpe County, which is adjacent to Athens-Clarke County. Ford called several other researchers and field investigators with whom he had made contact and done some research, and they came to the site to investigate with him. At least two of the men who came that day were trained trackers. The group stayed at the site until well into the night, and one of the trackers took photos of the print and the surrounding area.

At this sighting, the animal was said to have walked through farmland on its way south. Early in the morning hours, dogs belonging to residents who lived near the path the creature was walking on began barking wildly at the window. The residents did not see the creature, but did find prints and contacted the *Athens Banner-Herald*. The photos they took ended up on Wayne Ford's desk; that is when Ford and his team investigated.[159] In July 2007, one of the residents who had found the 2006 print saw the creature at the same location and called Ford. Upon investigation, Ford learned that there were two creatures at this time. Another resident who lived not far down the road from the woman who had called Ford reported that he heard a scream in the early morning hours and peered out the window. He had an outdoor light, which allowed him to see a tall, dark, hairy creature walk by. Ford went back to the area and stayed twice during the night. In his opinion, the fact that it had been there in April of 2006 and had come back in July 2007 meant that these creatures may have a pattern of returning to the area for food.[160]

In June of 2007, Ford was fortunate enough to take a tracking course under a trained, experienced tracker who also participated in Bigfoot research. It was a month after that course that he actually found his first footprint. He found the print along a path in the primary research area that he visits regularly. The print lay in a fire-ant mound along a path that hunters travel in that area. The creature had stepped in the mound on the human path. However, Ford did not feel that the creature was traveling the human path, but that it happened to step across the path while following its own course. Ford found other tracks where the animal had stepped on limbs and twigs. It had rained in this area just before he found the prints, making it easier to track the animal on that particular day. The animal seemed to be heading into a swampy area.

Ford made a measuring stick, as he had been trained to do in the tracking course he had previously taken. He used the stick to find each of the tracks over a length of about twenty yards. In the same direction, he found a dead tree of about four inches in diameter that the creature had broken in half — it was a fresh break. In addition, the animal had taken another dead tree three inches in diameter and about twenty feet in length, broken it, and laid it on the ground at a right angle. After spotting this, Ford traveled to the right of the tree toward a river. He felt like this was a main corridor of travel for the creatures in the area.[161]

A few days later, he was in another part of the forest going down a dirt road. He saw a tree bent and laid against another tree, and stopped his car to look at it. According to Ford, whatever had done this had stripped the tiny limbs off the tree. Nearby on a larger tree, something had stripped off the vines from the tree trunk and placed the smaller tree under the vine to hold it in place against the larger tree. Ford is not sure

Figure 4: In July 2007, a footprint was found along a path where something had stepped in a fire ant mound leaving a barefoot print larger than a size 11 boot. The trail led into a swamp. About 50 yards from the print, whoever or whatever had made that print laid this formation down on the ground with a dead tree.

what did this, but he did not feel that a human had made such a marker because it would have had very little purpose.

Figure 5: In the same time period as the previous picture and not far away, these two limbs were found laid side by side off a dirt road where another stick formation had been secured to a tree by a vine.

On another occasion in the same area of the forest in which he explores regularly, he found about six trees tied together and laid on the ground. This had not been there on his previous visit to those woods. While he has no definitive answer as to what did this, he feels that it looks suspiciously like Bigfoot activity. Bigfoot researchers all over the country frequently find similar markers. Some comment that Sasquatch often leave such things in their wake as messages or signs to other Sasquatch. These markers constituted the most activity he has seen in this area in a long time. He visits the area frequently, but oftentimes comes out of the woods with nothing in terms of Bigfoot evidence.[162]

Although he used to visit the woods a lot at night, he gradually cut back on his night visits. One night in the summer of 2007, he did go to the woods by himself. He set up camp in an area where an old house had once been. At that point, the only thing remaining of the old house was a set of concrete steps. He had a feeling that the creatures liked this area, so he wanted to explore there. On this visit, he heard whooping sounds in the vicinity. He commented that the hair on the back of his neck stood up. He started walking around the area and, shortly afterwards, he heard a rock hit the ground behind him. He turned on his flashlight, walking even closer to the site where the old house had once stood. There he heard what sounded like two of the creatures communicating with one another through more whooping sounds. He tried to join in, but the sounds stopped. He felt that he had disrupted what the creatures were doing.[163]

Ford has been privy to information from a good number of sightings in the northeast Georgia area. The latest and best evidence is a recent sighting in Georgia by a father and son. Ford was on the scene less than ninety minutes after the report came in. The father and son had seen the creature standing on the side of a rural road. Wayne searched for prints in the daylight hours. The father who had seen the creature was scared and did not really want to return to the scene. When he did come back during the daylight hours to help with the research, he brought a gun.

Before this encounter, Ford spoke with a union official from Atlanta who had come to hunt on land that had been rented from a landowner to establish a hunting club facility. One day, the union official was in a deer stand hunting, when he saw what he thought was a tall black man. He threw his scope up to get a better look, only to realize that he was not looking at a man. After a few seconds, the creature caught sight of the man and walked the other way. The man's son saw one on another occasion, and explained that he thought this one was a female. He and his father told the landowner, who retorted that the hunters should just leave the animals alone because they would not bother anyone. The landowner was told of the creatures a third time by another hunter who had also been part of the original land lease with the union official from Atlanta. Upon hearing of the sightings a third time, the landowner refunded the hunting group's money and made them abandon the property. Ford was able to contact the landowner, who allowed him to go on the property and look around. Ford indicated that upon talking to the landowner, he discovered that something had been killing his calves. In one instance, the landowner had sat and watched the area to try and figure out what was going on with his livestock. He left the "stake out" to return home to get more supplies, but when he returned another calf was dead. Ford feels that the creatures were actually watching the landowner, and when he left the area they got another calf, supposedly a food source for these creatures.[164]

To Ford, unusual structures and tree markers represent an interesting facet of the Bigfoot story. In January 2008, he went to the area he does research in where loggers had logged out two or three acres of forest. At a road near the logging site he found a few markers, some of them obviously not made by weather. In one, a dead tree had been put up high in another tree, and Ford did not think that weather had done this, and others who saw it agreed with him. He felt that the markers, if made by the creatures, were perhaps a result of the creature's reaction to the logging. He felt that they could have been a message to other creatures in the area or a response showing displeasure at the logging operations. Ford suggests that researchers should take note of logging activity going on in the forest.[165]

Although he has never seen one of the elusive creatures, Ford believes that they do indeed exist. He does not speculate as to what they really are, but believes that they are not currently chronicled by mainstream science. His goal in his research is simple: to collect evidence proving that the creatures exist and are living in the woods of northeast Georgia. He does not believe that a dead specimen is necessary to accomplish his goal — a clear, conclusive piece of video footage would do the trick. He has seen the Patterson/Gimlin footage, and, although he thinks it is genuine, he hopes his footage will be even more convincing. To that end, he travels to his private research area in the woods of northeast Georgia, usually on the weekends. Armed only with a video and film camera, he intends to continue to visit the area until he captures that piece of footage. As of yet, he does not have any footage of these creatures, but is quite hopeful that he will get his chance.

In his research, he has collected three reports that suggest the creatures are moving closer to urban areas. Three such incidents have already occurred that included sightings within one mile of the city limits of Athens, Georgia. He thinks that the animals are nocturnal and that they are drawn to certain things. For example, in many of the sightings he has heard of and researched, the animals have been sighted near chicken farms, which he speculates provide a source of food for them.[166]

Wayne Ford represents an anomaly in the mainstream media when it comes to Bigfoot. Most shrug their shoulders and attribute the stories, tracks, footprints, and unexplained noises to overactive imaginations and eager enthusiasts who will cling to any shred of evidence to prove that the creature exists. However, Wayne Ford has been and still is willing to follow the evidence all the way to its logical conclusion. In his opinion, there is something out there that people are seeing; the journalism and scientific communities cannot ignore that. There is too much evidence, according to him. He feels that all of the evidence needs to be examined.

Ford is willing to go the extra mile to examine the evidence, and he even goes out in search of his own. While many in the mainstream media do enjoy a good mystery, most will acknowledge that the Bigfoot phenomenon provides little more than an occasional opportunity to integrate news off the beaten path into the traditional media lineup. However, they go no further than this, especially the media in Georgia.

Very few serious journalists are willing to go as far as Ford has. Indeed he is correct when he says that most journalists report on Bigfoot sightings and the like in a cartoonish, humorous way. Even those who start off on a serious note often devolve into a comedic tone with a one-liner meant to elicit a chuckle from the reader and tickle the funny bone at the end. Ford, on the other hand, has remained true to his pledge not to put a humorous slant on his stories about the alleged creature. His work has been recognized by those in the Bigfoot field in general, as evidenced by his recent invitations to be a guest on two Internet radio shows broadcast all over the Web to talk about his experiences searching for the creatures in Georgia. While certainly there are those out there in the press and society in general who might poke fun at Ford's attempts or even berate him for bringing a serious light to Bigfoot phenomenon in Georgia, there are many out there who consider him to be more than commendable for his commitment to the truth and his attempt to solve the mystery. Whether the creatures exist in Georgia — or exist at all for that matter — one thing is certain: Ford has secured his place in Georgia sasquatchery.

7

Recent Reports and Encounters

The decade of the 1990s saw a fair number of sightings throughout the state. While sightings in Georgia's past have been mostly in the north Georgia area, particularly in the mountain region, more recent encounters indicate possible activity all over the state, although there are still a number of reported sightings in the northern reaches of Georgia and the Atlanta metro area. These modern sightings range from encounters where witnesses only had a few seconds to glimpse what they called a Bigfoot to encounters where the animal supposedly stalked and toyed with military personnel making their rounds and practicing maneuvers at state military bases throughout Georgia. There was even a rash of sightings in Coweta County, the area where the Belt/Belk Road Booger had charmed newspaper readers over twenty years earlier. The multitude of encounters and sightings that have surfaced in the last few decades can in part be explained by advances in communication, namely the Internet. Many of the stories below have been collected from Internet postings that, as was mentioned earlier, allow those who report the sightings a degree of anonymity. Whatever one might infer from the large number of sightings in the 1990s and the decade following the turn of the millennium, it is obvious that the legend of Bigfoot still persists in Georgia.

One of the earliest sightings of the 1990s happened in Lee County, Georgia, which is near the city of Albany in the southwestern corner of the state. The witness to this incident happened to be at the home of a friend with his brother and some friends. Not quite an hour after dark, the group of friends was standing in the driveway near the road. They noticed something come around the right side of the house. Assuming it had come across the creek that ran near the home, which was the only route through which the animal could have entered the area, they watched it walk around the yard as if it seemed comfortable with the surroundings. The figure they saw looked at least eight feet tall and appeared to weigh around four to five hundred pounds. It walked upright with a slight stoop, and the group noticed that the animal's shoulders were slumped, very wide, and covered with hair. The witnesses became so unnerved by what they had seen that they decided to retreat to one of the vehicles parked in the driveway, where they continued to watch the animal move around the yard. It walked to the left of the house and looked in the windows on that side before it disappeared into the woods.[167]

Young people were the witnesses for another encounter in 1993. This time the sighting happened in what seems to be the Georgia Bigfoot's most common terrain, the north Georgia mountains. That year, a recent high school graduate and three friends went to a well-known, local fishing area in White County to fish for trout. They parked their car on a dirt road running parallel to the river where they would be fishing. Two of the friends decided to try their luck fishing near the car, but the other two decided to fish up-river. A few hundred yards up an old roadbed, they came to a gully that seemed impassable. As they stood talking about a bridge that ought to have been there to allow vehicular traffic to pass, from behind them came a large thud. Turning around to investigate the noise, they noticed a ten-foot log in the roadbed. After deciding that the log could not have been there as they walked through due to its large size and the fact that they certainly would have seen it, they saw a Bigfoot standing about fifteen feet away. One of the witnesses described the animal as looking like "a big human covered in long, shaggy black hair." It was said to have a human-like face with dark reddish-brown eyes that appeared animal-like. The animal also looked as if it stood around nine feet tall, and it frightened them so much that the pair took off running as fast as they could.

When they arrived at their car, they directed the other two fishermen who came with them to gather their belongings so that they could all leave the area as soon as possible. When they were all back in the vehicle, they described their ordeal to the other two, who did not believe them at first but were unnerved at how frightened their friends had become. The main witness refused to return to the area for over three years, and, when he eventually did, he fished close to the vehicle and made sure he had panned the tree line for the creature. Around 1999, he did return to the exact place of the sighting, but was still uneasy and left quickly.[168]

In 1995, several members of the United States Army had a strange encounter with something stalking them as they were out on recon at Fort Stewart, Georgia, in the part that lies in Tattnall County, which is north of Savannah and one of the larger military installations in the state. The young men involved were assigned the task of doing a reconnaissance patrol with another unit also on the base. They did not have time to plan a route, so they struck out with only maps and a compass. Their route took them through swampy land and caused them to wade through water that was almost chest deep.

Upon exiting the swampy area, they could hear sounds indicating that someone or something was following them. At first thinking it was their instructors, they soon realized that no one would have been able to follow them, and, in addition, no one knew the route they were taking, so there was certainly no one already stationed along the route. For the next ten to fifteen minutes, whatever was stalking them would come close to them, drift off, cut to their right or left, and then come close again. They decided to break up into groups to see if the stalker could be confused. Instead, it started weaving between them in what the witness described as a figure-eight formation.

As they met back up, men from the different groups described hearing and feeling the same things as the others. Each of the soldiers became concerned at this point. Deciding to continue with their mission but taking a moment to check out the noises coming from the stalker, the soldiers lay facedown on the ground in the direction of the noises. A few moments later, whatever stalker was chasing them let out what the witness reporting the incident described as a "scream-roar." No one in the group had ever heard a sound like this, and they all looked at one another in bewilderment. Moments later, the unit heard another scream, followed by the sound of a tree falling and brush breaking. That was the end of the noises, and the soldiers felt as if their stalker had left the area. The soldier describing the incident indicated that he was a native of the mountains of West Virginia, an avid outdoorsman with much hunting experience, and was in his late twenties. At least one other soldier in the unit was described as being an outdoorsman with hunting experience. The men both claimed never to have heard screams like those before and felt that whatever had been stalking them was intelligent but did not want them there.[169]

Although these soldiers did not see their stalker, the descriptions they gave of the screams and the sounds of trees being pushed over and brush breaking is quite consistent with other reported encounters with Bigfoot creatures. Upon investigating the incident, Bigfoot Field Researchers Organization founder and leader Matt Moneymaker discovered that the soldiers could tell that whatever was stalking them was running in the woods on two legs, and that the screams were obviously coming from a large animal. The soldier told Moneymaker that the men in his unit were intimidated by how fast this stalker could move while it circled the unit without being spotted. The soldiers were carrying no large lights or spotlights, only small flashlights with red lenses suitable for reading maps, and had no night vision cameras, either.[170]

A few years later in May 1998, a police officer had an encounter with a creature that obviously enjoyed the solitude of Georgia mountain waterfalls much like he did. The location of this encounter was Rabun County at the edge of Minnehaha Falls. The officer was vacationing in the north Georgia mountains checking out Tallulah Gorge and other scenic wonders of the Georgia mountains, when he decided to visit Minnehaha Falls near Lake Rabun.

Making the quick hike to the falls, he noticed that he was the only one there, although there seemed to be a pungent odor lingering in the air that the witness described as akin to sweat. Shortly before nightfall, after the witness had sat down to enjoy a ham sandwich, he decided it was time to leave the area. Getting up, he noticed that there was someone else near the falls squatting down among some bushes. First thinking it was another hiker that he had either not seen or who had arrived quietly after his own arrival, he decided to walk over and say hello. It was then that the "other" visitor to the falls stood up, revealing a height of nine to ten feet. The witness thought that what stood up was just a very tall human until he got within twenty feet and could hear the thing breathing, sounding like someone who had a chest cold that caused rattling and gurgling sounds to emanate from the chest. He also began to smell a disagreeable odor as he drew nearer. At that time, the witness stopped and turned on his flashlight, but the animal walked away on two legs. It had dark brown hair that was matted in places.

Once it got about sixty feet away, it stopped and turned to look at the witness before taking about five or six steps in his direction. Being a well-trained police officer, the witness pulled his pistol and yelled at the creature to stop, which it did, then turned and walked away without turning back. Deciding he had seen enough of the north Georgia mountain wilderness, the officer left the area and drove back to his apartment in Marietta, perhaps feeling more comfortable within the confines of the city. When interviewed by a researcher from the BFRO, the witness said that the animal had a thick, short neck and very broad shoulders. He even commented that it reminded him of Darth Vader because of the way its neck sat on its shoulders.[171]

Fort Stewart seems to be a hotbed of Sasquatch activity. Just south of there in October of 1998, a hunter had a face-to-face encounter with what he called a Bigfoot. The man had been deer hunting, and had just climbed down out of his deer stand when he felt he needed to relieve himself on a nearby tree. It was at that time that he felt a strange calm in the forest. He mentioned that he heard no owls or coyotes, and he got a little alarmed at how quiet things were. Although his home was only a half mile away, he decided to try to leave the area as quickly as possible. It was getting dark and he could not shoot deer at night anyway.

He started walking and had just circled around a deadfall, when in his path about fifty or so feet away stood what he described as a Bigfoot. It stood eight feet tall, was covered with dark brown hair, had red eyes sunken into its skull, was hunched over, and its head sat on its shoulders with no evidence of a neck. The witness said that the creature's hair looked to be about an inch to an inch and a half long, and that its hair seemed longer on its buttocks and the back of its legs. The nose was flat with wide nostrils, and he said that although its head was small in proportion to the rest of its body, it was still large. When he first saw it, the creature appeared to have its head slightly cocked, sniffing the air, and the witness thought it did not see him at first, but shortly thereafter, the creature spotted him and stared directly at him.

The witness was carrying a twelve-gauge shotgun, but never felt threatened and was therefore not compelled to use the weapon. The two stood there staring at one another for about twenty seconds. The witness described the vicinity as having many ponds and bordering on several swamps; the area was full of pines. The man, who was a former member of the United States Armed Forces, became so unnerved after the incident that he moved his family from the area a week later. He also remarked that his wife, after he had told her of the incident, commented that the whole time they lived near those woods she had felt as if she were being watched. The witness also said that his dogs usually stayed under the porch unless he was outside with them. The man relocated to the Midwest shortly after the incident.[172]

Back in the north Georgia mountains, a glazier had a strange encounter in August 1999. While out taking measurements for a glass installation at a mountain property, the glazier noticed two Bigfoot-like creatures standing on an unfinished cabin balcony that overlooked a mountain near the town of Blue Ridge. One of the creatures was gray and the other was brown. He described the gray creature as seven to eight feet tall and the brown one as around seven. The man noticed that the two animals walked down the steps from the balcony leading to the wood line and then nonchalantly strolled into the woods on a trail. It looked as though the two had been using this trail to access and escape from the unfinished balcony for some time. A half hour later, the worker walked over and went inside the cabin, where he found sticks, twigs, tree limbs, and old clothing — all of which seemed to be used for bedding. At the time this report was made to the Gulf Coast Bigfoot Research Organization, the cabin had been finished and was occupied by the owners.[173]

The new millennium started off with a bang in terms of Georgia Bigfoot sightings. The creature was said to have been sighted on the Georgia/Alabama border, and it made an impression on two men that they will not soon forget. The encounter happened in early September 2000 and was first reported by a woman who was minding a BP Quick Stop in Alabama near Fort Mitchell. The clerk said that around 10:30 PM a young man came in the store requesting to use the telephone to call a game warden. The clerk described the young man, who looked to be about eighteen years old, as "petrified." While in the store, he told the clerk that he and a friend, a man in his thirties or forties, had recently fled from Rood Creek Park, which is a small campground in Georgia across the Chattahoochee River from Alabama. The campground also includes a boat-landing area. The young man stopped at the BP because it was the first place he found on his route away from the campground.[174]

The frightened teenager described his ordeal to the clerk. He said that he and his friend "had been camped at Rood, when his dog, a yellow Labrador retriever, suddenly started making weird noises. It wasn't like the dog was barking; it was more like the dog was screaming or crying. So he went to check on the dog, and, when he did, he heard something big coming through the woods."

As the attacker grew closer, the witness could see that it was much bigger than he was, and he himself was six feet tall. He said the thing towered above him, but he did not make a detailed description of it. He was unnerved and pulled out his pistol, firing several rounds directly at the creature to no effect. The young man said that the animal took his dog, and then later said it had "tore his dog up."

The frightened young man called a game warden from the store, and the warden asked if the two men would go back to the area to look around with an officer, a request that he flatly refused. After the phone call, he returned to his car and left the store. The clerk said that the young man had parked his car, which appeared to be a Ford Mustang with an Arkansas license plate, very close to the entrance to the store and directly under a light. The older man stayed in the car and would not get out. Also while in the store, the young man said that the two had been so frightened that they fled the area hurriedly without taking time to collect their camping equipment — a story that checked out when another customer in the store decided to go to the area to look around and found their camping equipment right where they had left it.

The reporter covering the story went to the area himself and talked to a few campers who had been in the vicinity on more than one occasion close to the time of the sighting, and they claimed to have seen and heard nothing, but several people interviewed said that the report did not surprise them, for they mentioned that one can often see strange things in the area. One person interviewed even mentioned that there are locations in nearby Alabama where people have reported seeing a strange hominid during the evening hours.[175]

In the summer of 2001, an Indian artifact hunting trip turned up much more than the man looking for arrowheads had expected. On July 28, 2001, while looking around for any Indian artifacts he could find, a man came to a wooded area alongside a creek in Cherokee County. He claimed to have startled something standing on the other side of the creek. Whatever it was started running away from the creek area, and the man knew from the sounds it was making as it fled that it was very large. Not thinking too much of the situation, the man turned to leave the creek and return to the vicinity near his car to continue hunting for arrowheads. At this point, he felt that he was being watched, a sensation that is commonly reported in a Bigfoot encounter. About thirty minutes later, he began to smell a foul odor, which prompted him to look around to see if there was a deer carcass nearby. Then, something let out a yell. The yell sounded like a tropical bird at first, but then went to a very deep human-sounding tone, but much louder and deeper. Less than a minute later, another yell came in from the opposite direction, like it was answering the first yell. This yell was more human, with more grunt sounds. The man seemed to be in between them, and he decided not to run, but to return to his car instead. After leaving, he vowed never to return to the area alone or without a gun.[176]

Later that year, in December 2001 at the opposite end of the state, a Florida resident got the shock of her life as she crossed a bridge on the Clyattville Road in Brooks County while returning home in the early morning hours. As the lady was driving home, she approached a bridge on the dark rural road and saw what she thought was a man standing near the side of the bridge. Fearing that the man might wander into the road and get hit by her oncoming car, she flashed her lights. Getting no response from the figure, she tapped her horn, but noticed that the figure did not walk away or move away from the road. Instead, it seemed to reach for something beside the road, perhaps leaves on a tree.

She decided to slow down, fearing that it was a drunken man who might wander out into the road, but as she drove by she was horrified at what she saw. She described it as looking like a giant human with a shaggy fur coat, or perhaps a huge animal. She saw that it stood on two legs, and as it turned its face toward her car, it dropped one of its arms down to its side revealing that its arms were very long. Its eyes glowed red as the lights from her car hit its face.

The witness was alone and there were no other cars on the road. What she saw frightened her so much that she hit the gas and drove very quickly the rest of the way home. Not wanting to be branded as a "kook" — crazy — or risk her professional reputation, the witness did not mention her sighting to anyone but her husband, which she only did several weeks after the incident. She commented in her report to the BFRO that she was very frightened by what she saw, and although she would gladly talk to anyone who wished to follow up on her sighting, she

did not want her name or profile mentioned in relation to the sighting —
a common request from those who have had a frightening experience
associated with Bigfoot.[177]

In November 2003, a young man and his father were setting up tree
stands on family owned property in Coweta County, when the son
spotted tree limbs as thick as a man's wrist that were broken and snapped
off some fifteen to twenty feet off the ground, as well as an overturned
rock that was four or five feet wide by three feet tall. Concerned about
the possibility of bears in the area, he decided to mention the incident to
his grandfather, who had considerable hunting experience in the area.
After talking with his grandfather, he learned that in the twenty-plus
years that he had been hunting, there had never been any bear signs that
he knew of in Coweta County.

Later that evening, the young man returned to the hunting area and
started to climb his deer stand when he smelled a foul odor in the air, a
smell he likened to old garbage. He climbed his stand and awaited a deer.
He had a clear view of an area lying below a power line. While sitting
quietly in his stand, he heard a deer approaching. He looked over his
shoulder to see a doe running by as if it had been spooked. After lifting
his gun to peer through the scope and see what had spooked the deer, he
spotted what looked like a human, but was eight feet tall and had a
"cinnamon-dark brown hairy body." The young hunter said it cleared the
opening in just one stride. It had very broad, square shoulders and its
arms hung down low by its side. While it moved through quickly, the
young man knew it was not another hunter. The young man was so
unnerved by what he saw that he never hunted in those woods again, and
he even commented that his family never talks about what he saw that
day in the woods.[178]

One of the most intriguing Bigfoot sagas in modern Georgia history takes us again to the woods and neighborhoods of Coweta County. In addition to the above sighting, Coweta is also the home of the legendary Belt Road/Belk Road Booger reported in the summer of 1979 and discussed earlier in this work. The county saw another rash of Bigfoot-like sightings in the spring and summer of 2005. Like the Belt/Belk Road Booger, the sightings of what has become known as the Happy Valley Horror were covered by the local paper, the *Times-Herald*.

Reporter Alex McRae, in his first article about the encounters, asked the question: Has the nightmare returned? McRae reports that a tip to the paper from a man who identified himself as an avid hunter and outdoorsman reported a huge beast that was very hairy and walked upright across

Figure 6: Happy Valley Circle near the Madras Community in Coweta County. This was the road on which many sighted a creature that walked upright and was called "The Happy Valley Horror."

a field on Happy Valley Circle. A recent trip to Happy Valley Circle by this writer and a fellow researcher born and raised in the area revealed that Happy Valley Circle is indeed a circular road that winds through a wooded area in a community called Madras, not too far from the county seat of Newnan. The area borders Lake Redwine, and has become a very popular location for rural subdivisions and large homes. The area is beautiful with its green rolling hills, heavily forested areas, nice homes, and a creek that runs through the woods.[179] The man who reported the first sighting from this area indicated that what he saw scared him to death. He wanted to know if the paper had received any other reports from area residents describing anything that might resemble a Bigfoot.[180]

In his report, McRae interviewed the sitting sheriff of Coweta County, Mike Yeager. According to Yeager, their office had not reported any encounters at the time of the initial report to the paper, but declared

Figure 7: Did "The Happy Valley Horror" roam these woods?

that his office was prepared to deal with whatever problem might occur in the area, including Bigfoot.

McRae also reported that, according to research, most Bigfoot sightings happened near streams, creeks, or other bodies of water. As mentioned earlier, Lake Redwine is on Happy Valley Circle, which according to McRae offers enough water to support a large Bigfoot population. Nevertheless, at the time of the report, no residents near Lake Redwine had reported sighting a large, hairy creature. One interesting note, however, was that the area seemed to be lacking its usual armadillo population, an animal suspected to be a favorite food of Bigfoot. One resident interviewed for the article mentioned that he used to have to watch out for armadillos while driving home from work in the area, but, since St. Patrick's Day, he had not seen one in the area.[181]

Figure 8: Wooded area off Happy Valley Circle.

As news reports of Bigfoot sightings often do, McRae's first report caused quite a stir, so much so that McRae had to write a follow-up piece a month later on May 25, 2005.

This time, the report took on an even more lighthearted tone. Entitled "Women Set Trap for Bigfoot," the article concerned two local women who were quite concerned about sightings in their backyards. They devised a plan to prove that the whole thing was a hoax. Jan Brice Stout, one of the two women, mentioned that her family had owned land on Happy Valley Circle for the past four decades; the other resident, Beth Greene, had lived in the area for over twenty years. Both women wanted the public to know that their area was not the home of a wild hairy beast.

Figure 9: Creek running parallel to Happy Valley Circle. Did the "Happy Valley Horror" creature refresh itself with water from this creek?

To prove this, Stout planned to lure the animal with her beef stew and was sure that Bigfoot, if he was real, could not resist that. Greene planned to lure the creature with her famous Happy Valley Circle Pecan Pie. She was certain that would work, claiming, "Nobody's ever turned this down."

The two admitted that they were just having a lot of fun with the whole thing. Stout even joked that she had heard that Bigfoot walked around naked, and to help him cover his nudity, she had a "pair of giant-sized under-drawers donated by her employer, Belk of Newnan."

Although these ideas seem a little on the jovial side, there was a practical, more serious side to their actions. With the release of the first article by McRae, crowds of curiosity-seekers and Bigfoot buffs had

Figure 10: Another view of the creek running parallel to Happy Valley Circle.

been coming to the area wanting to get a good look at the community's elusive, yet famous, resident. Stout even reported seeing strange vehicle tracks on her property, which meant that uninvited visitors had been making themselves welcome to walk around on private property looking for something that might or might not be in the woods. She had even had a few coming right up to her driveway and then fleeing when they caught sight of her.

Greene reported that after the story was released in the paper and on the companion Internet site, her niece, who works as a conservationist in the Lake Tahoe, California, area, reported that a California Bigfoot specialist with whom she was acquainted was very tempted to head out

Figure 11: From this picture, it is easy to see that Happy Valley Circle is developing quickly. Has this new development displaced a creature that once roamed the area?

to Georgia to check out the reports and look for the creature himself. Greene commented, "He was ready to catch a plane and come out here... Thank goodness we talked him out of it." The two women even mentioned that they hoped to organize a local community celebration to honor what many called the Happy Valley Horror. The festival was to be held in Newnan on the courthouse square, and Stout mentioned that she was even trying to recruit a local radio station as the event's sponsor. According to Stout, the event would draw interested parties to the city, where local merchants could benefit from sales and a portion of the festival's proceeds would go to charity. There was talk of a Bigfoot look-alike contest. The festival has yet to happen.[182]

All was quiet on Happy Valley Circle for the next few months, but, in September, the Happy Valley Horror made a comeback. This time, he was even said to be causing traffic problems. According to Donna Robards, a lifelong resident of Coweta County, she and her husband laughed at the reports of the creature when they first came out in April of that year. But something happened that changed her attitude.

It happened on August 22, 2005, when her son Jeff, who at the time was 18, saw the creature while returning home on Happy Valley Circle where he lived with Donna and her husband. After dropping off his sister at her home in the east Coweta area, he headed home on Cedar Creek Road near the place where it intersects Happy Valley Circle. It was around 2:30 in the morning, and as he approached the stop sign, he was shocked to see a huge, hairy creature walking in the middle of Cedar Creek road, and it was coming toward his vehicle. Jeff described the creature as big, hairy, and walking upright. At first thinking it was a bear, Jeff left the area quickly, but after talking to his mother, he began to doubt that possibility, for the animal had a flat face and did not have a snout like a bear. The two were perplexed and could not figure out what Jeff had seen.[183]

Donna Robards would not have long to wonder about her son's encounter, for three days later on August 25th, she would see firsthand the very sight that had so unnerved her son. Right before midnight that night, as she was driving home after working late on her job in LaGrange, Robards was heading north on Happy Valley Circle when she reached the Cedar Creek intersection, much as her son had three nights before. There, she saw two of the creatures as they stood in the road a few yards ahead of her. She quickly hit the brakes and skidded to within twenty feet of the hairy duo. She described the larger of the two creatures as eight feet tall and covered with black hair that looked coarse; the second animal was shorter and its hair appeared to be reddish-brown. The smaller one ran off into the woods when Robards came to a stop, but the taller one turned and walked right toward her. The thought of this animal coming toward her car and possibly reaching right inside and grabbing her made her frightened beyond belief. Fortunately, the creature stopped and started off into the woods after the smaller one. Robards described the animal as apelike, not human, saying, "It stood upright, but the hair on its face was shorter than on the rest of its body. And the eyes didn't bulge like an ape's. They were set back like human eyes."

After pondering the incident, Robards said she did remember that she and her husband had returned home in March 2003 several times to find items missing. Perhaps the items had been taken by the Happy Valley Bigfoot? She was not sure, but thinks it could be possible. Robards and her family do not live too far from Lake Redwine. They mentioned that the animals seen by her and her son were all headed in the direction of the lake when spotted. Robards is still concerned about the possibility of seeing one of the creatures in the road again. According to the report, Robards said, "I am always careful to look for deer when I'm on the road... But now I'm going to be even more careful. Whatever that thing was, I sure don't want to run up on it again."[184]

Word of the sightings began to spread and even attracted the attention of a television station in Columbus, a city with a population of over a hundred thousand located on the Georgia and Alabama border right down Interstate 85 from Newnan. Reporter Jon Kalahar of WTVM went to the area to report on the sightings. Interviewing Alex McRae, who wrote the stories for the *Times Herald* in Coweta County, Kalahar discussed the reliability of the witnesses with him. McRae commented that, "These are reliable people. They're hard-working, honest people with no reason to make these things up, and these incidents we're talking about happened months apart, so it's not like someone said I just heard this — let's get in on the action." Kalahar also interviewed Sam Rich, who founded the Georgia Bigfoot website and has spent years investigating Bigfoot sightings in Georgia. According to Rich, "There's a natural trail right through [the area where the sightings are reported]." He further commented that he "thinks it strengthens the argument and definitely points to the fact that the phenomenon is worthy of research. But whether or not there's actually a large undiscovered animal out there is something were still trying to find out."[185]

The sightings continued to bring interest, this time from a former resident of Coweta County who planned on filming a documentary on the subject as part of his senior thesis at the Savannah College of Art and Design. Andrew Marshall, who grew up in Coweta County and graduated from East Coweta High School in 2003, was a long-time film student and enthusiast even before going on to SCAD. Deciding to pursue a career in the field of documentary production, Marshall decided to do a documentary about the Bigfoot phenomenon in Georgia, and his main interest in the documentary was the people who claim to have seen the creature rather than the creature itself. He contacted people in Coweta County and the surrounding areas of Georgia who had reported seeing Bigfoot, and made contact with researchers and organizations that track the animal around the state.[186] Marshall did produce the documentary, but mainly focused on researcher Sam Rich, with whom he traveled to the north Georgia mountains to film Rich as he conducted research and searched for Bigfoot evidence. When asked about his experience during the project, Marshall, who is now an associate producer of *Georgia Outdoors* for Georgia Public Broadcasting, told me that after meeting Sam Rich, he believes that if everyone would approach their research like Sam, we would have an answer to the mystery one way or the other. "Sam wasn't so quick to identify a sign as a possible Sasquatch. He was very meticulous with his research and conducted it very thoroughly." Marshall also commented that his professors were glad to accept his documentary as his senior thesis, and that besides it helping him earn his degree, the project was a lot of fun.[187]

A few years later on April 1, 2008, the Happy Valley Horror was still in the headlines of the *Times-Herald*, but this time it was not a reported sighting, but rather an April Fools Day prank by the paper. In an article entitled "Happy Valley Group Concerned School Will Harm Bigfoot Habitat," Alex McRae fooled readers into believing that the construction of a Coweta County elementary school had a local environmentalist group up in arms because it was believed that the construction of the school would destroy the Bigfoot's habitat. The story mentioned that the school was being built on Jim Starr Road, a road that dead-ends on

Happy Valley Circle and also runs right over the creek pictured in the photos taken by Susan Prosser and me. The story was quite elaborate and included lines from previous articles and quotes from experts, law enforcement officials, and the naming of a fictitious group called Save the Happy Valley Horror. The report ended with a brilliant quote: "People talk about wanting to save the world... Why not start right here at home? It may be a Horror, but it's our Horror and it deserves to be saved." There is even an address to which readers could write if they desired additional information. Everything looked in order, but the last line of the article had this in parenthesis: "(The preceding was a special April Fool's Day report.)"[188] It seems that the Happy Valley Horror may indeed have gotten to be a bigger part of Coweta County legend than the Belt/Belk Road Booger ever had.

One of the most startling reports comes from Paulding County, a suburban Atlanta county on the southwest side not far from Coweta County. This incident took place over a span of several days in June of 2006. While there are a number of credible eyewitnesses in Georgia who report seeing something, the following report, when I showed it to a couple of my colleagues in the scientific community, caused them to stop and ponder. The encounter took place in a subdivision not far from the town of Hiram. The man who made the report had been living in the area with his girlfriend and dogs for quite some time, when they were awakened one night by an intruder that rendered his dogs useless in terms of protecting the property. The man, who was quite large himself and had at one time been a nightclub bouncer, was awakened around 1:30 AM by the sound of his dogs barking frantically at something in the woods. He felt that it was either a deer or another dog, for in the ten years he had lived on the property, he never seen or heard of a person in the woods behind his home. When he went outside and the dogs quieted down as a result of him scolding them, he could hear footsteps in the distance, and he distinctly remembers them not being of the four-legged kind. He went on to describe the incident:

> I went back inside to grab a flashlight and my 9mm pistol, but as I went back in the door I heard a sort of scream/shriek. It was very loud and actually made me jump a bit. I was thinking it was likely teenagers at this point, likely shouting some sort of insult, but there was something unnerving about the way it carried into my home. I told my girlfriend, who was stirring back to being awake, that there was somebody walking in the woods making weird noises and that she needed to come hear it for herself and I was going to run them off. I ran back onto the porch and shouted, "Whoever you are, I am going to let these dogs out so you'd better speak and be on your way!" No response came back, but the footfalls were obviously close to the fence line and were heavy sounding. I went over to the gate and the dogs would not leave the yard or my side. This is the first time ever that I have witnessed them refuse a chance to run in the woods. At this point I was a bit angry and embarrassed that I had made a threat to the intruder and the dogs just stayed put.[189]

After this, the man yelled another verbal threat, and to his surprise the intruder moved from one end of the yard at his fence to the other in less than fifteen seconds. He decided it was time to stop speaking and start shooting, so he took his pistol and fired three rounds into the ground. This drew another scream from the animal, and the sounds of its footsteps indicated that it was coming closer to side of the house where the man was standing. At this juncture, the man's girlfriend was out on the porch between him and the woods. She became frightened herself and decided to go back inside. The movements and screams of this creature had the witness — a 6'4", 290-pound man — shaking in fear, not a small feat. He decided to retreat nearer to the door of his house when he heard the creature's footsteps as it walked back into the woods. The witness's girlfriend had not entirely gone back in the house and was standing in the doorway. Both of them then heard whatever animal this was smash trees together in sets of three, making a sound that the witness said sounded like "whump" each time. He felt that this was the animal's way of letting him know that he knew the man had fired three gunshots, hence the sounds coming in sets of three.[190]

At this point, the man's girlfriend was pleading with him to come inside, but the witness was not satisfied with what he had heard. Hoping it was just a bunch of teenagers pulling a prank, he yelled back at the intruder requesting him to identify himself. This brought the animal back out of the woods. The witness decided he needed to get a camera from inside in the event that the animal showed itself where he could catch it on tape. He went to the side porch with his camera and he could hear the animal move closer to him, seemingly walking near the fence line. Each time the man moved, the animal seemed to move with him. After a while, he decided to go back inside, when he heard what sounded like his dogs in the shed in his back yard, but he was horrified when he got back to the door and saw that his dogs were inside and not in the shed. The dogs were cowering in fear and had to be physically moved to the porch, something that had never happened before. Still feeling frightened and not wanting to take any chances, the witness went to his workroom, where he grabbed a thick piece of wood to prevent the back door from sliding open. He commented that the whole time he had lived there, he had never even had a lock on the back door because the dogs were so reliable in keeping anyone who was not family away.[191]

The next day, the man decided to run lighting along his fence-line and buy a high-powered spotlight in case his visitor returned. After returning home from a hardware store, he and his girlfriend were out at the fence discussing what they planned to do when the man caught sight of the animal. Between two trees and some brush he saw what appeared to be three feet of black fur. His girlfriend looked up in time to see the bushes part. The animal seemed to "duck-walk" away into the woods. Later, the two found a footprint about fifteen inches long that showed a heel and toes. They also found a strange black substance bubbling up from the ground nearby in their yard, which the witness mentioned, may have drawn the creature to the area.

An investigator from the BFRO, Leigh Culver, a trained and professional tracker, came to the site and interviewed the man and his girlfriend. Finding both to be very credible, Culver wanted to look at the area where the witness had seen the patch of fur. The man described the fur as like that of an Irish setter and wavy. As they took measurements, Culver hypothesized that the patch of fur the man saw would have been at least five feet off the ground from where it stood. In addition to the print found by the witness, Culver found another print measuring twenty-one inches long and nine inches wide. He also mentioned that the area of the sighting was near Sweetwater Creek, and that the area had a history of sightings dating back as far as thirty years from the time of this particular incident.[192]

Returning to the north Georgia mountains, Lumpkin County near the city of Dahlonega was the site of an encounter involving two lovebirds and a creature that came too close for comfort in autumn, 2006. A couple parked on a rural road in the nighttime hours decided that they would take advantage of the opportunity to take in some night air, and they got out of their truck and began walking, hand in hand. It was a beautiful moonlit night, and as the campers walked, the man with a flashlight in hand, they both began to smell a skunk. After a short while, the smell turned into a rotten garbage smell. Not far up the road, the two decided to turn around and head back to the truck. That was when they saw a large, hairy creature that stood eight to nine feet tall and looked as if it weighed somewhere around five hundred pounds. The animal stood there gazing back at them, and moved its head back and forth like an owl. It did not move toward them, but just stood there glaring back at them. The sight scared them so much that the woman began screaming, which obviously frightened the creature, for it took off very quickly and disappeared, taking only a couple of steps. The couple, still unnerved at what they had seen, quickly made their way back to their truck, walking right through the area where the creature had stood.[193]

On December 18, 2006, a small group of friends had a nighttime encounter with a Bigfoot creature in Haralson County near the Georgia and Alabama border. In the vicinity of the settlements of Draketown and Buchanan, six adults were driving around on one of the passenger's property. They had just left a cookout at the family cabin, when they saw a herd of deer leave a pasture area and flee into the woods. The witness mentioned that it was strange to see this, because the deer usually knew that headlights were followed by the throwing out of corn, which the owners of the property did frequently. As they turned a corner closer to one of the pastures, they saw a "large, black, two-legged creature" cross a dirt road. Once it had seen the lights of their vehicle, it turned and ran into an area of thick pines. They saw a being that was at least as large as a grown human man, walked on two feet, and had weird-looking long arms. They said that the animal was black and was wearing no clothes.[194]

In February 2007, longtime Bigfoot researcher Sam Rich finally had a Bigfoot encounter in the north Georgia mountains, where he has long conducted research. Sam Rich, who began the website www.georgiabigfoot.com and was involved in Bigfoot field research in the northwestern part of the state before moving from Georgia due to employment, relayed to me that he had always been interested in the subject of Bigfoot. A fan of movies such as *The Legend of Boggy Creek* and *The Creature from Black Lake*, he did not become actively involved in Bigfoot research until he was in his twenties. After living in the Pacific Northwest for a time, he moved back to Georgia in 2002, made contact with individuals from the Gulf Coast Bigfoot Researchers Organization, and accompanied them on a trip where they found evidence of the creature, including a footprint. Rich also had rocks thrown at him by some unseen force, and right before dark he had an encounter with something in the brush. All these things got him hooked on Bigfoot research in Georgia, and the website he founded stemmed from that trip.[195]

The encounter happened as Sam Rich and film students from the Savannah College of Art and Design were in the area producing a documentary about the Sasquatch phenomenon in the state, part of the same film project that Andrew Marshall was conducting that I mentioned in conjunction with the Happy Valley Circle sightings. Rich had just eaten dinner and was setting up a camera on a tripod for use later in the evening. The film students were still cooking their meals when Rich saw the creature. The men were located near a food plot that had been maintained by the Georgia Department of Natural Resources for quite some time. Rich was setting up the camera on the tripod in his vehicle and was looking to position the camera properly. He looked up and saw a large, black, bipedal creature passing from his left to right along the back of the food plot. Rich described the creature saying:

> The head was set very low to the shoulders. The shoulders blended into the back of the head, which went up in a line parallel to the angle of the back and ended in an obvious point or crest. The head then sloped back down to the forehead. The chin was either tucked into the chest or very low in comparison to the shoulder. It gave the impression of blending straight up from the front of the torso to the face. The overall build was robust but not massive. The arms were long. The legs appeared proportionate to the body, but seemed short in comparison to the arms.[196]

Although there was not much physical evidence left at the area where the sighting took place, investigators who helped follow up on the report from Rich did find that his story seemed credible and he seemed sincere. In his email to me, Rich indicated that this has been his only visual encounter up to now.[197]

The fact that sightings in Georgia have taken place right up to the present indicates that the legend and story of Bigfoot still persists, and there is much to talk about in the state in terms of current field investigations and Bigfoot research. As indicated, the modern sightings have taken place all over the state of Georgia, but there is no denying that a preponderance of sightings has taken place in the north Georgia area, specifically areas in and around metro Atlanta. The north Georgia mountains also continue to be a popular location for Bigfoot sightings.

Researcher Mike Bankston of Georgiabigfoot.com says that he thinks there are a lot of sightings in these locations because of human encroachment. He does not think there is a huge population of the animals, if they exist, but does say that areas with the more recent sightings in the north Georgia area are getting heavily populated, and people are living and building more and more in areas that used to be virtually unpopulated. He mentioned that although the mountains in the northern part of the state do provide better coverage as far as forest is concerned, there is a lot of building and development going on there as well.[198]

I can at least attest to the fact that the Happy Valley Circle area in Coweta County, site of the Happy Valley Horror sightings from 2005, is still a heavily wooded area but is seeing a great deal of housing development. There are quite a few new subdivisions along that stretch, and there are plenty of homes that appear to have been built there within the past few years, possibly giving some credence to what Bankston said in terms of human encroachment being a possible cause for the multitude of sightings in a given area. This encroachment, coupled with the possibility of the animal's existence and the fact that there is some evidence of violent interactions, leads me at least to think that there is some merit to furthering investigation into the possibility of humans sharing the terrain with these creatures. As in contact with any other species, there could be ramifications, and that very idea is the subject of the next chapter.

Conclusion

No one can deny the fact that Georgia is a growing state, as thousands of people relocate to the area each year. As recently as 2008, Georgia made the Forbes list of the top ten fastest-growing states. The Atlanta metropolitan area, as one might expect, has seen most of that population growth, but not all of it. Census officials have reported over the years that most of north Georgia is growing, as well as areas in central Georgia, specifically around Macon and Warner Robins, and the coast of Georgia has gained population, as well. While this population growth is not evenly distributed throughout the state by any measure of the imagination, what is obvious is that people are moving to all parts of Georgia. One visit to the north Georgia mountains and one will see just how this region is becoming not only a top tourist destination, but also the destination of those seeking a peaceful and serene place to raise a family or spend their twilight years. Georgia is very attractive to people looking for an escape from the colder climates of the Northeast and Midwest. The real estate market is good in Georgia, with homes reasonably priced for a state with a large metro area like Atlanta, a historical Mecca like Savannah, the Atlantic shorefront along the Barrier Islands, and the beautiful mountain vistas of the Blue Ridge. So what does all this mean for the legendary creature that many say lives in the Peach State along with all these newcomers and natives?

Clearly, it means that there will be more and more human traffic in areas where there once was none. As subdivisions begin to dot the landscape of Georgia, more and more natural resources will be taken up by the quest to build more dwellings for all those coming to the state to live or those moving around the state. Environmentalists and conservationists in Georgia have been shouting for a while now about the vanishing countryside and wooded areas in so many parts of north Georgia. Interestingly enough, there are a number of wetlands and habitat preserves in the state located right next to major highways and interstates. Henry County in the southern part of the Atlanta metropolitan area has allocated space for such places. So it is obvious that population growth in Georgia is going to have an impact on its wildlife, including the legendary creature.

From this, one can only conclude that it is important to try to learn the truth about Bigfoot, not just in Georgia, but everywhere. However, our topic is just the Peach State, and as the chapters on historical and modern sightings bear out, studying the possible existence of these creatures in Georgia is not such a wild idea. Historical sightings of the mythical animal in Georgia can be traced as far back as the early 1800s.

Scientists and field researchers have staked their reputations on the existence of these animals, and they swear that they exist in Georgia, too.

As Matt Pruitt pointed out in his many conversations with me, these animals are just like any other. They must eat, and with their supposedly enormous size, they must eat a lot. This means that the creatures will need an abundance of the same types of food that bears and other commonly seen Georgia animals eat. However, it appears that they do not or cannot forage for food in the same manner as deer and bear — they must forage under the cover of darkness. This could be a good thing. As these animals might have figured out, foraging for food and being active at night leads to less interaction with humans, but as more and more humans move into territory once used by these creatures, contact will be inevitable, whether at night or during the day.

Pruitt maintains that there are no modern reports of a Bigfoot hurting anyone. However, as he makes very clear, these are animals that will defend themselves if they are attacked or threatened. While there are no modern reports of Bigfoot attacks in Georgia, there are a few from the early 1800s through the mid-1900s of Bigfoot-like creatures chasing or pursuing humans, but most of these incidents happened as a result of humans stumbling upon a Bigfoot or tromping through Bigfoot territory or foraging grounds. There are a few of these stories included here in this book. The same kinds of reports exist in Tennessee and Florida, suggesting that it is quite possible to be harmed by these creatures. As I have pointed out, there are indeed instances where these animals have wandered onto the property of humans, and some have even been brave enough to venture close enough to human homes to peek into windows and doors. In Texas, one must remember the frightful boyhood encounter of Bobby Hamilton, founder of the Gulf Coast Bigfoot Research

Organization. I am certainly not trying to insist that these animals are the cold-blooded killers that the low budget Hollywood film industry portrays; I am merely making an observation about what has and could happen as a result of Bigfoot and human contact. If these animals do indeed exist in the manner that Dr. Jeffery Meldrum, Dr. Grover Krantz, Matt Pruitt, Bobby Hamilton, Matthew Moneymaker, Steve Hyde, Mike Bankston, Wayne Ford, and others feel they do, then the topic does merit further study.

There seems to be no stopping the continual growth and expansion of the human population in Georgia. The movement into the state by Americans from other places coupled with immigration from places like Mexico and India means that Georgia will eventually be bursting at the seams. Its cities will grow, leading some to move or retire to quieter, more rural parts of the state. This will definitely lead to encroachment on lands occupied by wildlife and necessary to the hunting and foraging of wild creatures — including Bigfoot. If these creatures have the strength and physical capabilities that some who have encountered them have reported, then danger is possible and even unavoidable in some instances. Further study could lead to a number of outcomes.

First, scientific study on a large scale can help put the mystery to rest. People are definitely seeing something. Many stories about Bigfoot are obviously fraudulent or jokes. In 2008 in metro Atlanta, two hoaxers with obviously very little knowledge of science and history tried to convince the world they had found a Bigfoot. Their story was widely reported, but, as it turns out, they had purchased a Halloween costume and frozen it in a chest-style freezer. I spoke with the two men involved, and I can report that their activities have certainly damaged Bigfoot research as a whole, especially in Georgia. However, many witnesses are credible and have no reason to lie about what they have seen. There might be a creature in the woods of Georgia that science hasn't acknowledged yet. Discovery of new species is certainly not anything new. Late in 2008 dozens of new species were discovered, adding to the already endless pages of species chronicled by zoologists and biologists. It really is not hard to imagine that a new species of ape could exist undiscovered by scientists. One need only think of the giant panda, the Komodo dragon, and even the mountain gorilla to understand how some of our knowledge of the animal kingdom has come about only recently. No one knew these creatures existed, despite reports from travelers who had caught glimpses of them in their natural habitats. Universities and colleges should be eager for an opportunity to have the potential vault of knowledge that the discovery of Bigfoot could open.

Second, if these animals are discovered and found to live and interact with their environment the way researchers hypothesize they do, good scientific research could answer a lot of question about how these animals survive and how they can peacefully coexist with an ever-expanding human population. While I realize that it would be hard to keep these animals in natural preserves and limit their movement outside of national and state parks where hunting is illegal and human settlement prohibited, it might lead to answers regarding their migratory patterns or whether they migrate at all. Setting aside land is not a bad idea, but what is an even better idea is to try to understand their feeding, social, and travel habits. Bigfoot researchers constantly argue about what foods these animals do and do not eat. Some say they are herbivores, while others argue that they are omnivores. Good scientific analysis might lead to an answer to that question.

Third, research could possibly lead to answers we need about the animal kingdom itself. Research could begin with "How?" Yes, how. How did these animals come to be? How did they go undetected by the general human population for so long? It might be possible to understand how these animals are able to avoid human contact on so many levels, and how they are able to almost blend in with their environment. Bigfoot exhibits a lot of human characteristics. How is he able to live peacefully in nature and with the animal kingdom?

Finally, we would have an answer to the pivotal question: "Is Bigfoot a hominid or primate?" There are powerful voices on both sides of this argument. There are places in the United States where state and local laws forbid the hunting and killing of these animals. Some of those who have passed laws like this argue that they are animals and need to be protected for future study, or simply as are other animals for which protective laws are already in place. Others have pushed for the passage of such laws because they believe these animals are more human than anything else, arguing that killing these creatures would be like killing another human. Then, of course, there is the theory that these animals are a missing link and could fill in a gap on the human evolutionary chain. All of these ideas are more than plausible, and research should be conducted on a large scale.

Inspection of the U.S. budget in any given year will turn up thousands, sometimes millions of dollars appropriated for the minutest of scientific projects. Federal monies are spent on researching the growth pattern of certain types of frogs, the easiest way to raise brine shrimp, mule museums, bridges to nowhere, and the feeding habits of pets. Also, one must consider NASA, the National Aeronautic and Space Administration. While there are a number of things that federal money is used for by NASA, one of those things is the search for potential life in the universe. To many, the argument is more than valid that if taxpayers fund the search for extraterrestrial life, some tax dollars could be used to fund a search for the North American great ape.

It is obvious that the legend of Bigfoot has a substantial presence in Georgia. Sightings of these creatures go way back to the times of the early settlers of Georgia, and the argument can be made that both Creek and Cherokee legends reflect interaction with a being we now call Bigfoot or Sasquatch. When most think of Bigfoot, they think of Washington, Oregon, or California. Rarely do they think that these animals could exist in Georgia, or anywhere else for that matter. But as history shows, Bigfoot could call the Peach State home. Perhaps you, the reader, have seen or heard something that might be the legendary creature tromping through the woods of the deep Georgia forests. It is a subject that deserves more attention. And now I leave it to you, with the evidence in hand, to decide what to make of these reports of a huge, hairy creature living in the state of Georgia.

Endnotes

[1] Loren Coleman. (2003). *Bigfoot: The True Story of Apes in America.* New York: Paraview Pocket Books. 66.

[2] Coleman, *Bigfoot: Apes in America,* 32.

[3] Norma Gaffron. (1989). *Bigfoot, Great Mysteries: Opposing Viewpoints Series.* San Diego: Greenhaven Press, 23-25.

[4] Carrie Carmichael. (1977). *Bigfoot: Man, Monster, or Myth?* Austin, Texas: Steck-Vaughn Publishers. 18.

[5] Carmichael, *Bigfoot: Man, Monster,* 21.

[6] Janet and Colin Bord. (2006). *Bigfoot Casebook Updated: Sightings and Encounters from 1818 to 2004.* Enumclaw, Washington: Pine Winds Press. 8-9.

[7] Gaffron, *Bigfoot,* 28-31.

[8] Carmichael, 40-41.

[9] Gaffron, 34-37.

[10] Ibid, 39-41.

[11] Jeff Meldrum. (2006). *Sasquatch: Legend Meets Science.* New York: Forge, 133-34.

[12] Greg Long. (2004). *The Making of Bigfoot: The Inside Story.* New York: Prometheus Books. 453.

[13] Coleman, *Bigfoot,* 100.

[14] Matt Pruitt, interview by author, 30 July 2008.

[15] Matt Pruitt, interview by Robert W. Morgan, Blogtalkradio,

http://www.blogtalkradio.com/THEAARFSHOW, 20 December 2007
[16] Matt Pruitt, interview by author, 30 July.
[17] Ibid.
[18] Ibid.
[19] Ibid.
[20] Matt Pruitt, interview by Robert W. Morgan.
[21] Ibid.
[22] M. Pruitt, interview by author, 30 July 2008.
[23] Ibid.
[24] Meldrum, *Sasquatch: Legend Meets Science*, 89-90.
[25] M. Pruitt, interview by author, 30 July.
[26] Meldrum, 96.
[27] Pruitt, interview by author, 30 July.
[28] Ibid.
[29] Pruitt, interview by author, 8 August 2008.
[30] Pruitt, interview by author, 30 July.
[31] Ranger, interview by author, 20 December 2007.
[32] Pruitt, interview by author, 30 July.
[33] Ranger, interview by author, 20 December 2007.
[34] Philip L. Rife (2000). *Bigfoot across America*. Lincoln, Nebraska: Writer's Club Press, 44.
[35] Pruitt, interview by author, 30 July.
[36] Ibid.
[37] James Mooney. (1995). *Myths of the Cherokee*. New York: Dover Publications, 16-40.
[38] Claudio Saunt, "Creek Indians," *New Georgia Encyclopedia*, http://www.newgeorgiaencyclopedia.com. (accessed 12 December 2008)
[39] Saunt, "Creek Indians."
[40] Sam Riley, "A Search for the Cultural Bigfoot: Folklore or Fakelore?" *Journal of Popular Culture 10*:2, 377-87.
[41] Daniel Littlefield. (1992). *Alex Posey: Creek Poet, Journalist, and Humorist*. Lincoln: University of Nebraska Press, 25.
[42] Troy Parkinson and Dale Bosch, "Swamp Beast," Monster Quest, The History Channel. 26 December 2007.
[43] Mooney, *Myths of the Cherokee*, 338.
[44] Mooney, 338-40.
[45] M. Pruitt, interview by author, 8 August 2008.
[46] Mooney, 479.
[47] Ibid, 480.
[48] Ned L. Irwin, "John Haywood," *The Tennessee Encyclopedia of History and Culture*, http://www.tennesseeencyclopedia.net. (accessed 1 January 2009)
[49] Mooney, 418.
[50] Pruitt, interview by author, 8 August 2006

[51] Georgia Historical Marker at Blood Mountain, Georgia Historical
Commission, Marker Number 144-3, 1958.

[52] Pruitt, interview by author, 8 August 2006

[53] James C. Cobb. (1997). *Georgia Odyssey*. Athens: University of Georgia
Press, 10-12.

[54] Chad Arment. (2006). *The Historical Bigfoot*. Landisville, Pennsylvania:
Coachwhip Publications, 127.

[55] C. Arment, *Historical Bigfoot*, 127-28.

[56] "Swamp Beast," Monster Quest, The History Channel, 26 December 2007.

[57] Jim Miles. (2006). *Weird Georgia*. New York: Sterling Publishing Company,
23.

[58] "A Wild Man in Georgia," *New York Times*, 10 February 1883: 5.

[59] Arment, 131-32.

[60] Ibid, 132.

[61] "The Wild Man of Tennessee," *New York Times*, 8 February 1889: 1.

[62] "Fayette Sightings/Encounter," Gulf Coast Bigfoot Researchers Organization,
http://www.gcbro.com. (accessed March 6, 2008)

[63] "An Oberon-ish Outlaw," *The Lafayette Advertiser*, 21 August 1889,
http://www.bigfootencounters.com/articles/jones_countyGA.htm. (accessed
6 March 2008)

[64] "Archives of Greene County Historical Society Recall," *Herald-Journal*, 5
October 2001, p. 10.

[65] "Bridgeboro Terrorized by Mysterious Beast," *Atlanta Constitution*, 9 August
1906.

[66] Philip L. Rife, *Bigfoot across America*, 53-54.

[67] "Thomas County Georgia," Bigfoot Encounters,
http://www.bigfootencounters.com. (accessed 11 March 2008)

[68] Bord, *Bigfoot Casebook Updated*, 61-62.

[69] "Report 6097," The Bigfoot Field Researchers Organization,
http://www.bfro.net. (accessed 11 March 2008)

[70] "Report 8405," The Bigfoot Field Researchers Organization,
http://www.bfro.net. (accessed 11 March 2008)

[71] "Oregonbigfoot.com File #00812," Oregonbigfoot.com: The Legend Lives...,
http://www.oregonbigfoot.com. (accessed 11 March 2008)

[72] "Oregonbigfoot.com file #01119," Oregonbigfoot.com: The Legend Lives...,
http://www.oregonbigfoot.com. (accessed 11 March 2008)

[73] "Report 447," Bigfoot Field Researchers Organization, http://www.bfro.net.
(accessed 11 March 2008)

[74] "Effingham Sightings/Encounters," Gulf Coast Bigfoot Research
Organization, http://www.gcbro.com. (accessed 11 March 2008)

[75] "Report 14525," The Bigfoot Field Researchers Organization,
http://www.bfro.net. (accessed 11 March 2008)

[76] Winston Skinner, telephone interview, 19 March 2008.

[77] "Strange Creature Seen Here," *Times Herald*, 9 August 1979, front page section.

[78] Skinner, telephone interview.

[79] "Belt Road Booger is Seen Again," *Times Herald*, 16 August 1979, front page section.

[80] "Booger Sighted at Sargent," *Times Herald*, 23 August 1979, front page section.

[81] Alex McRae, "Could Bigfoot be in Coweta?" *Times Herald*, 24 April 2005.

[82] Skinner, telephone interview.

[83] McRae, "Could Bigfoot be in Coweta?"

[84] Skinner, telephone interview.

[85] Alex McRae, "Another 'Bigfoot' Sighting in the Happy Valley Area," Times-Herald, 17 September 2005.

[86] Skinner, telephone interview.

[87] "Macon County Georgia, Oglethorpe," Bigfoot Encounters, http://www.bigfootencounters.com. (accessed 11 March 2008)

[88] Rife, Bigfoot across America, 54-55.

[89] "Report 9712," Bigfoot Research Organization, http://www.bfro.net. (accessed 11 March 2008)

[90] Janet and Colin Bord, *Bigfoot Casebook*, 182-83.

[91] "Franklin Sightings/Encounters," Gulf Coast Bigfoot Research Organization, http://www.gcbro.com. (accessed 11 March 2008)

[92] Steve Hyde, telephone interview by author, 21 December 2007.

[93] Sam Rich, "Elkins Creek Revisited," 16 September 2006, http://www.georgiabigfoot.com. (accessed 20 December 2007)

[94] S. Hyde, interview.

[95] James Akin quoted in Sam Rich, "Elkins Creek Revisited," 16 September 2006, http://www.georgiabigfoot.com. (accessed 20 December 2007)

[96] Hyde, interview.

[97] James Akin quoted in Sam Rich, "Elkins Creek Revisited."

[98] Ibid.

[99] Hyde.

[100] Ibid.

[101] Tom Paulson, "A student of Sasquatch, Prof. Grover Krantz, dies," Seattlepi.com, http://www.seattlepi.nwsource.com/local/58730_grover18.shtml. (accessed 21 January 2008)

[102] Hyde.

[103] Dr. Jeffrey Meldrum, interview by Ira Flatow, Lexis Nexis, 10 November 2006, http://www.lexisnexis.com/us/lnacademic/results/docview/docview.do?risb=21_T2880861815&format=GNBFI&sort=RELEVANCE&startDocNo=1&resultsUrlKey=29_T2880861818. (accessed 4 January 2008)

[104] Dr. Jeffrey Meldrum, telephone interview by author, 4 January 2008.

[105] J. Meldrum, telephone interview.

[106] Ibid.

[107] Hyde.

[108] Hyde.

[109] "Fingerprint Expert Tries to Debunk Bigfoot—Reaches Opposite Conclusion." *Houston Chronicle*, 2000. 23 Dec. 2007 http://www.bigfootencounters.com/articles/chilcutt.htm.

[110] Jimmy Chilcutt, "Dermal Ridge Examination Report: Georgia Casting," http://www.georgiabigfoot.com. (accessed 20 December 2007)

[111] Hyde.

[112] Ibid.

[113] Meldrum, telephone interview.

[114] Gwendolyn Driscoll, "PART I: They're on a mission to find Bigfoot in California," *Orange County Register*, 4 December 2007.

[115] G. Driscoll, "Bigfoot in California."

[116] Ibid.

[117] "About the Bigfoot Field Researchers Organization (BFRO)," Bigfoot Field Researchers Organization, http://www.bfro.net/REF/aboutbfr.asp. (accessed 10 February 2008)

[118] "About the Bigfoot Field Researchers Organization."

[119] Gwendolyn Driscoll, "He's on a mission to find Bigfoot... near Lake Tahoe," *Orange County Register*, 5 December 2007.

[120] Jeffrey Meldrum, *Sasquatch: Legend Meets Science*.

[121] Meldrum, *Sasquatch*.

[122] Ibid.

[123] "About GCBRO," Gulf Coast Bigfoot Research Organization, http://www.gcbro.com. (accessed 24 February 2008)

[124] Mary Lee Grant, "Bobby Hamilton hunts the hairy beasts that he swears haunted him as a kid," *Houston Press*, 3 March 2003.

[125] M.L. Grant, "Bobby Hamilton."

[126] "About GCBRO," Gulf Coast Bigfoot Research Organization.

[127] "Sightings/Encounters," Gulf Coast Bigfoot Research Organization, http://www.gcbro.com. (accessed 24 February 2008)

[128] Mike Bankston, "Georgia Bigfoot," email to author, 22 December 2007.

[129] Steve Hyde, "Evolution of a Blobsquatch, Another Illustration," Georgia Bigfoot, http://www.georgiabigfoot.com. (accessed 24 February 2008)

[130] Steve Hyde, telephone interview, 21 December 2007.

[131] Hyde, interview.

[132] Ibid.

[133] Georgia Swamp Ape Research Center, http://www.forteansociety.tripod.com/crypto1.html. (accessed 24 February 2008)

[134] Wayne Ford, interview by Robert W. Morgan and Jim Helbert, Blogtalkradio, 29 November 2007, http://www.blogtalkradio.com/THEAARFSHOW. (accessed 25 January 2008)

[135] Wayne Ford, telephone interview, 28 December 2007.

[136] Jeff Meldrum, _Sasquatch_, p. 19.

[137] Ford, telephone interview.

[138] Ibid.

[139] Wayne Ford, "Georgia's Swamp Ape, Fact or Fiction?" _Athens Magazine_, April 2001.

[140] Ford, "Georgia's Swamp Ape."

[141] Ibid.

[142] Mike Bankston, "Georgia Bigfoot," email to author, 22 December 2007.

[143] Ford, "Georgia's Swamp Ape."

[144] Ford, interview by Robert W. Morgan and Jim Helbert.

[145] Ford, interview by Morgan and Helbert.

[146] Wayne Ford, interview with Darin (Thunderhawk) and J. C. Johnson, Blogtalkradio, 27 January 2008, http://www.blogtalkradio.com/the_bigfoot_mystery. (accessed 2 February 2008)

[147] Ford, telephone interview. See also, Wayne Ford, interview with Robert W. Morgan and Jim Helbert.

[148] Wayne Ford, "Tales of Bigfoot include sightings in Georgia—even Clarke County," _Athens Banner-Herald_, 13 Dec. 2003.

[149] Wayne Ford, "Tales of Bigfoot."

[150] Ford, "Tales of Bigfoot."

[151] Ibid.

[152] Ibid.

[153] Wayne Ford, "Truisms or tales? Bigfoot book addresses both," _Athens Banner-Herald_, 13 Dec. 2003.

[154] Michael J. Carson, "The Bigfoot Film Controversy," Reviewers Bookwatch, May 2005. Findarticles.com, http://findarticles.com/p/articles/mi_mORGU/is_2005_May/ai_713760933. (accessed 3 Feb 2008)

[155] Wayne Ford, "Bigger than life: New book further explores sasquatch question," _Athens Banner-Herald_, 3 Oct. 2004.

[156] Wayne Ford, "Bigger than life."

[157] Ford, telephone interview.

[158] Wayne Ford, "Fact or Fiction on the hunt," _Athens Banner-Herald_, 12 February 2006.

[159] Ford, telephone interview.

[160] Wayne Ford, interview with Robert W. Morgan and Jim Helbert.

[161] Ibid.

[162] Ibid.

[163] Ibid.

[164] Wayne Ford, interview with Darin (Thunderhawk) and J. C. Johnson.

[165] Ibid.

[166] Ibid.

[167] "Report 18707," The Bigfoot Field Researchers Organization, http://www.bfro.net. (accessed 11 April 2008)

[168] "White County Sighting/Encounter," Gulf Coast Bigfoot Research Organization, http://www.gcbro.com. (accessed 11 April 2008)

[169] "Report 4109," The Bigfoot Field Researchers Organization, http://www.bfro.net. (accessed 11 April 2008)

[170] "Report 4109."

[171] "Report 9818," The Bigfoot Field Researchers Organization, http://www.bfro.net. (accessed 5 April 2008)

[172] Report 5395," The Bigfoot Field Researchers Organization, http://www.bfro.net. (accessed 5 April 2008)

[173] "Gilmer Sightings/Encounters," Gulf Coast Bigfoot Research Organization, http://www.gcbro.com. (accessed 6 April 2008)

[174] Tim Chitwood, "Seen a Bigfoot Lately?" *Columbus Ledger-Enquirer*, 13 September 2000.

[175] Tim Chitwood, "Seen a Bigfoot Lately?"

[176] "White County Encounters/Sightings," Gulf Coast Bigfoot Research Organization, http://www.gcbro.com. (accessed 6 April 2008)

[177] "Report 4393," The Bigfoot Field Researchers Organization, http://www.bfro.net. (accessed 12 April 2008)

[178] "Report 15457," The Bigfoot Field Researchers Organization, http://www.bfro.net. (accessed 11 April 2008)

[179] The author visited the area on April 3, 2008 with Susan Prosser, who assisted in gathering information for this book from the Coweta and Fayette County areas. We drove the length of Happy Valley Circle, stopping regularly to look at areas along the road and take pictures of locations where animals might wander and look for water and food. The pictures of Happy Valley Circle included were taken by Mrs. Prosser on that trip.

[180] Alex McRae, "Could Bigfoot Be in Coweta?" *Times Herald*, 24 April 2005.

[181] Alex McRae, "Could Bigfoot Be in Coweta?"

[182] Alex McRae, "Women set trap for Bigfoot," *Times-Herald*, 22 May 2005.

[183] Alex McRae, "Another 'Bigfoot' Sighting in the Happy Valley Area," *Times-Herald*, 17 September 2005.

[184] Alex McRae, "Another 'Bigfoot' Sighting."

[185] Jon Kalahar, "Is there Bigfoot in Georgia?" WTVM.com, http://www.wtvm.com/Global/story.asp?S=4906451&nav=8fap. (accessed 23 December 2007)

[186] Alex McRae, "Have you seen 'Bigfoot?'" *Times-Herald*, 27 November 2006.

[187] Andrew Marshall, telephone interview, 18 March 2008.

[188] Alex McRae, "Happy Valley group concerned school will harm Bigfoot habitat," *Times-Herald*, 1 April 2008.

[189] "Report 14887," The Bigfoot Field Researchers Organization, http://www.bfro.net. (accessed 1 November 2007)

[190] "Report 14887."

[191] Ibid.

[192] Ibid.

[193] "Georgia Couple face 9 foot tall, 500 pound Goliath on dark road...," Bigfoot Encounters, http://www.bigfootencounters.com. (accessed 13 April 2008)

[194] "Report 18377," The Bigfoot Field Researchers Organization, http://www.bfro.net. (accessed 11 April 2008)

[195] Sam Rich, "Research on Georgia Sasquatch," email to author, 12 March 2008.

[196] "Report 67," Sasquatch Research Initiative, http://www.sasquatchonline.com. (accessed 14 March 2008)

[197] Rich, email to author.

[198] Mike Bankston, "Georgia Bigfoot," email to author, 22 December 2007.

About Jeffery Wells

A 10th-generation Georgian, Professor Jeffery Wells is a Georgia historian who has written articles on notable Georgia figures such as Major Archibald Butts and former Senator Paul Coverdell. He holds a bachelor's degree in history from the University of Georgia, where he graduated *cum laude* in 1996, and a master's degree in history from Georgia College & State University in Milledgeville where he was the Dr. William Ivey Hair Outstanding Graduate Student in History for 2006.

Professor Wells is a veteran teacher, having been in the classroom for 12 years, three of which have been in the college classroom. He currently serves as the social sciences and education department chair for Georgia Military College's Atlanta campus where he teaches courses in American, world, religious, African-American, and Georgia history. Before becoming a professor, he taught at the middle school, high school, and technical college levels. He has also served on a local public school board in Georgia.

In addition to his teaching, Wells is a member of the Georgia Association of Historians, the Southern Historical Association, the Genealogical Society of Clayton and Henry County, the Historic Oakland Foundation, the Old Campbell County Historical Society, the National Museum of Patriotism, Georgia's Old Capital Museum Society and Robert Penn Warren Circle. An avid fan of Georgia mysteries, he maintains a blog site devoted to chronicling the mysteries and strange phenomenon in Georgia. The site can be found at www.georgiamysteries.blogspot.com. In addition, he has made guest appearances on several radio shows discussing his blog site and historical research including the Dr. William Lester Show. He is also a contributor to the McDonough Haunted History Tour in McDonough, Georgia where he lives.

In 2008, Wells was named Georgia Military College's Character Educator of the Year by GMC President Major General Peter J. Boylan.